Basic Bible Sermons on the Church

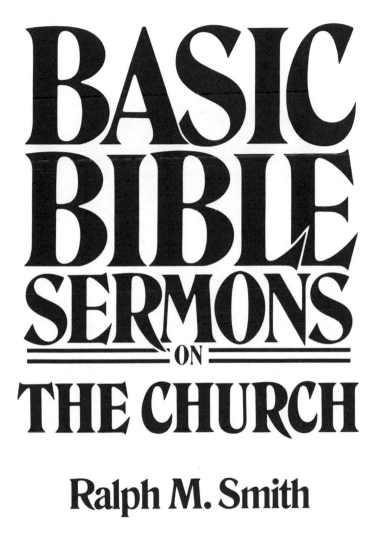

BASIC BIBLE SERMONS

ON

THE CHURCH

Ralph M. Smith

BROADMAN PRESS
NASHVILLE, TENNESSEE

Unless otherwise indicated, Scripture is from the *King James Version*. References marked RSV are from the *Revised Standard Version of the Bible* copyright 1946, 1952, © 1971, 1973 by the National Council of the Churches of Christ in the U.S.A., and used by permission.

Library of Congress Cataloging-in-Publication Data

Smith, Ralph M., 1931-
    Basic Bible Sermons on the Church / Ralph M. Smith.
        p.   cm.
    ISBN 0-8054-2275-7
    1. Church—Sermons.   2. Baptists—Sermons.   3. Southern Baptist
Convention—Sermons.   4. Sermons, American.   I. Title.
BV600.2.S575   1990
262—dc20   89-78454
                                                                CIP

To
Wayne and Mary Louise McDonald
faithful friends and dedicated Christians
who have encouraged my wife, Bess, and me

Contents

Other Books in the Basic Bible Sermons Series:

Basic Bible Sermons on the Cross, W. A. Criswell
Basic Bible Sermons on Easter, Chevis F. Horne
Basic Bible Sermons on John, Herschel H. Hobbs

1
The Invincible Church

(Matt. 16:13-25)

A London newspaper offered a prize for the best essay on the subject: "What is wrong with the church?" The prize was won by a minister from Wales. He gave this answer: "What is wrong with the church is our failure to realize and wonder at the beauty, the mystery, the glory, and the greatness of the church."

The church is God's one redemptive institution placed on this earth. It was to the church that Jesus gave the Great Commission. It is through the church that Jesus brings the message of salvation to the world. It is for the church that Jesus one day will return.

Never forget that the church with all its faults will stand until Jesus comes again. Jesus promised that the gates of hell will not prevail against the church. The church is invincible!

What makes Christ's church invincible? How has the church been able to stand for nearly two thousand years? Why has Satan with all of his schemes failed to defeat the church? Why have humans been unable to destroy the church? What makes the church invincible?

I. The Church Is Invincible Because of the Transformed Nature of Its Membership

Every member of the church is to be a transformed individual. He or she is to be a child of God through faith in Jesus Christ. Jesus explained this to His disciples as He was with them at Caesarea Philippi.

Our Lord knew that His days in the flesh were numbered, and He knew some would not understand Him. Was there anyone who recognized Him and who would carry on His work after He ascended to heaven? That was the crucial problem. It involved the very survival of the Christian faith.

In a dramatic scene Jesus asked His disciples, "Whom do men say that I the Son of man am?" (v. 13). Here was a homeless, penniless Galilean carpenter with twelve ordinary men. At that very moment, Jesus' death was being plotted.

Notice where Jesus chose to ask the question. The area was scattered with temples of the ancient Syrian Baal worship. By Caesarea Philippi there arose a great hill. In it was a deep cavern said to be the birthplace of Pan, the Greek god of nature. In Caesarea Philippi, there was a tremendous temple of white marble built to the Roman godhead of Caesar. Jesus stood at the center of Syrian, Greek, and Roman worship. There, of all places, he asked, "Who do you say that I am?" (v. 15, RSV). Peter clearly stated the deepest conviction of his soul, "Thou art the Christ, the Son of the living God" (v. 16). What a statement! Christ means "the anointed one" and refers to the work Jesus came to do as messianic deliverer. "Son of the living God" has reference to the deity of Jesus. Jesus is God incarnate.

Simon Peter said two glorious things about Jesus: as to His work, he said Jesus is the anointed Messiah. As to His person, Peter stated that Jesus is God come in the flesh.

Even so today, that church is invincible where members have confessed their belief in Jesus Christ as the Messiah who is God! This is the essential work of the church. We preach the gospel, "for it is the power of God unto salvation to every one that believeth" (Rom. 1:16).

The single most important prerequisite for being a member of a local New Testament church is the new birth. The invincible church has a regenerated church membership through faith in Jesus Christ.

Rembrandt could take a piece of canvas, dab his paints on it, and create a beautiful painting. We call that art. Shakespeare could write a sonnet or a play on a sheet of paper. We call that genius. John D. Rockefeller could sign his name at the bottom of a check, and it was worth millions of dollars. We call that capital. A skilled workman can take a piece of metal, shape it, twist it, mold it, and it becomes a thing of usefulness and beauty. We call that craftsmanship. But only

God in heaven can take a sinner and make a saint! We call that salvation. The invincible church has a transformed membership.

II. The Church Is Invincible Because of Its Dynamic Relationship to Christ

After Peter made his great confession regarding his faith in Jesus, our Lord said: "Upon this rock I will build My church; and the gates of hell shall not prevail against it" (Matt. 16:18). This is a beautiful promise that Jesus gave to His church. The thrust of the statement is that the church is invincible because of its dynamic relationship to Jesus Christ.

First, the church is built on Christ. Jesus said, "You are Peter, and on this rock I will build my church" (v. 18, RSV). Here we have a play on words. Jesus said, "You are Peter [*petros,* a small stone]. On this rock [*petra,* a gigantic boulder, or foundation stone], I will build my church." The rock on which the church is built is the person of Christ Himself. The church is built on its Founder, the divine Son of God, not on Peter. The apostle himself told us in 1 Peter 2:4-6 that Jesus is the chief cornerstone of the church. The Bible says that no other foundation for the church can be laid except Jesus Christ (1 Cor. 3:11). The hymn writer was correct when he wrote, "The church's one foundation/Is Jesus Christ her Lord." You and I are placed in the church as living stones so that we can do spiritual services that are acceptable to God (1 Pet. 2:5).

Second, the church is built by Christ. Our Lord said, "Upon this rock *I will* build my church," (author's italics). Not only is the church built on Christ, but the church is built by Christ. Nineteen hundred years ago, Jesus walked the shores of Galilee, the towns and cities of Israel, calling forth fishermen like Peter, James, John, and Andrew. He saved a tax collector named Matthew. He found a zealot named Simon. He discovered a woman at the well and gave her the water of life. Jesus was building His church. Dramatically one day, He turned to His disciples and said, "Ye have not chosen me, but I have chosen you" (John 15:16).

It is in the providence of God that you are living in this century and that you are a member of your church. This is not by luck, chance, or accident. The same Christ who chose Peter, Andrew, James, and John chose you, saved you, and placed you in His church that you might serve Him.

Since God has placed you in His church, that means at least two things. First, it means God has a place of service for you. You are to love the church and give yourself to it as Christ loved the church and gave Himself for it. Second, it means that you and I must not reject those that Christ has chosen. We are to love the people of the church.

A number of years ago, a young associate pastor came to me complaining about a lady in our church. He felt that she was sometimes more critical than she ought to be. As a matter of fact, she had given our young associate pastor a rather difficult time. I said, "Don't criticize that lady. She is the most valuable member in our church."

Rather astonished, he responded, "Why do you say that she is the most valuable member in the church?"

I smiled and said, "She is teaching you a great lesson. If you can learn to love her, you can learn to love anybody."

One day a visitor approached the great British pastor Charles Hadden Spurgeon. Spurgeon inquired why the visitor had not united with the church. The man responded, "I started to join the church, but I looked around, and I saw a hypocrite. I decided not to join."

Spurgeon, who had a quick wit, said to the man: "In the first church the leader, Simon Peter, cursed. One apostle, Thomas, doubted the resurrection. The treasurer, Judas Iscariot, betrayed the Lord. The first church was not perfect! Furthermore, I have never seen a church that is perfect. But, sir, if you ever find the perfect church, please do not join, for when you become a member it will no longer be perfect." The church is being built by Jesus, and you and I should accept those whom the Lord has placed in His church.

Third, the church is successful only through Jesus' power. After Jesus told the disciples He would build a church, He made this great promise, "The gates of hell shall not prevail against it"! When I first read that statement, I thought of the church as being shut up like a fortress with the forces of hell attacking the church. Upon closer scrutiny, I discovered that the passage taught just the opposite. Jesus said that the gates of hell could not prevail against the church. The church is attacking the gates of Hades. As the church carries out its evangelistic ministry by sharing the gospel, we batter down the gates of hell and death. As the church preaches the gospel, we snatch the lost from a burning hell that they would receive if they rejected Christ as their Savior.

The Lord here is commanding us to be an attacking army sent from heaven. "Go ye into all the world, and preach the gospel" (Mark 16:15). The theme song of the church is not "Hold the fort!" but rather, "Onward, Christian soldiers"!

It takes faith to make a church great. Faith is the confidence, the assurance, the belief in God and His power. We can become what God wants us to be. We can do what God would have us to do. When we set out to do what God would have us to do, there will be people at every crossroad on the highway of success who will say, "It cannot be done." They do not have the faith, they do not have the vision. We must not allow them to rob us of our faith and our vision to attack the gates of hell. Great things are possible if we dream great dreams for God.

I like the spirit of the three survivors of a wrecked ship in the Pacific. These men landed on a lonely Pacific island. Scouting over the island, they found no other humans there. It was a barren sort of an island just a mile or so in diameter. When Sunday came, the three men met and had church. They discovered they were all Christians. Before they dismissed on Sunday, they set a goal to have four in church the following Sunday. I like that spirit. Great things will happen if we will believe.

"I will give unto thee the keys of the kingdom of heaven: and whatsoever thou shalt bind on earth shall be bound in heaven: and whatsoever thou shalt loose on earth shall be loosed in heaven" (Matt. 16:19). Greek scholars call this a future paraphrastic construction. It means: Whatever we bind on earth *shall have already been bound* in heaven! Whatever we loose on earth *shall have already been loosed* in heaven! Jesus told us to receive our orders from God in heaven. We have the keys of the kingdom, and we can unlock the gates of hell. On the Day of Pentecost, Peter used these keys of the kingdom, and three thousand people were loosed from the gates of hell. In Acts 10, he used these keys again, and the household of Cornelius was converted.

In striking metaphors, the New Testament describes the main task of the church. Jesus compared the Christian to light, salt, water, bread, and fire, and He told us that we have the keys of the kingdom of heaven. Now, what can light, salt, water, bread, fire, and keys have in common? Penetration is the one common denominator. Light penetrates darkness, and it disappears. Salt penetrates meat, and it is preserved. Water penetrates the ground, and a harvest springs forth. Bread penetrates the body and gives strength. A key penetrates a lock, and a door is opened. And fire is dependent on penetration for its very survival.

The church of Jesus Christ is God's penetrating force in our society. As Christians move in society, they are to preach the gospel (Mark 16:15). We are to bring the world to the foot of the cross that men and women might know Christ as Lord and Savior. The church is invincible that has this unique relationship to Christ.

III. The Church Is Invincible Because of the Unique Way in Which It Does Its Work

Immediately after announcing how He would build His church, Jesus explained that He must die and be resurrected. Not fully understanding, Peter objected. Jesus rebuked him and then announced the eternal principal for building a great Spirit-filled church: "If any man will come after me, let him deny himself, and take up his cross, and follow me" (Matt. 16:24).

A. Self-denial

The church is invincible when we deny self. This means that we enthrone Christ as we dethrone self. Christians should remember that we never bless unless we bleed. A candle never gives light until it is consumed. Water does not become steam until it is put under 212 degrees of heat. Grapes have to be crushed before they become juice. Wheat has to be ground before it becomes bread.

Christ is the Savior because He died on the cross. Jesus taught that self-denial is the key that opens the door to success in Christian service.

B. Cross-bearing

Our Lord taught that the church is invincible when we take up our cross. The Christian life is the sacrificial life. Luke, in his Gospel, added one word to this command: "Let him deny himself, and take up his cross *daily*" (Luke 9:23, author's italics). A life lived in the constant hourly awareness of the demands of God and the needs of others is more important than moments of sacrifice.

The great Christian Sundar Sigh was traveling with a Tibetan companion on a bitterly cold day. As they trudged through the mountain, they felt they could not survive the terrible experience. Reaching a steep precipice, they saw a man who had slipped over the edge. The man was almost dead on the ledge of the rock below. Sundar immediately went down to try to help the poor fellow to safety. The companion refused to help saying that it would be all they could do to save themselves and went on, leaving Sundar behind.

With great difficulty, Sundar managed to get the dying man up the slope and back on the road. He struggled along, holding the man up. Before long, they came upon the body of his former companion. The Tibetan was frozen to death.

On struggled Sundar, and gradually the dying man, receiving warmth from the friction of his body against that of his rescuer, began to revive. Sundar himself grew warm through his labor. At last, they reached the village and were safe. With a full heart, Sundar thought of the words of the Master, "Whosoever will save his life shall lose it: and whosoever will lose his life for my sake shall find it" (v. 25).

The church is invincible only as we follow Christ. Jesus said, "Follow me" (Matt. 4:19; Mark 2:14) The Christian must render to Jesus Christ perfect obedience.

2
Jesus in the Midst

(John 20:19-23)

Jesus had conquered death, and by the mighty power of God He had been resurrected from the grave. The disciples were gathered in a house behind locked doors. Jesus walked through the doors and stood in their midst. This is the first church building where the resurrected Lord was in the midst of His people.

"Then . . . came Jesus and stood in the midst" (v. 19). That is the essence of the Christian faith: Jesus in the midst of human life. Moreover, this is the theme of the Bible:

in Exodus, Jesus was "in the midst of the earth" (8:22);

in Deuteronomy, He was in the midst of the camp to deliver Israel (23:14);

Jeremiah exclaimed, "Thou, O Lord, art in the midst of us" (14:9);

Daniel reported Jesus was in the midst of the fiery furnace with Shadrach, Meshach, and Abednego (3:25);

as a babe, Jesus was in the midst of the shepherds and the wise men;

as a boy, He was in the midst of the doctors of theology in the temple;

as God the Holy Spirit, Jesus is in the midst of His people where two or three are gathered together (Matt. 18:20);

at Calvary, Jesus was in the midst of sinners: "Where they crucified him, and two other with him, on either side one, and Jesus in the midst" (John 19:18);

as a Lamb in Revelation, Jesus is in the midst of the throne of God;

as our resurrected Lord, Jesus is in the midst of the churches (Rev. 1:13).

On the evening of the first Easter Sunday, Jesus "stood in the midst" of His disciples (John 20:26). Why is this theme repeated? Because this is the key to the Christian life.

This is the key to the abundant life.

This is the key to the fellowshiping life of the church.

This is the key to the witnessing life of the believer.

And this is the key to the successful life of any child of God.

Thus, as we assemble in the house of worship, our deepest desire is that Jesus will be in our midst! As a matter of fact, you can have Jesus in the midst of your life. There are some people who have *no room* for Christ. There are others who have *some room* for Christ. Jesus wants *every room*. He told His disciples to go and find an upper room, furnished, ready for the Master.

Here we find Jesus in the midst of His people. No Christian can be spiritual, powerful, or growing unless Jesus is in the midst of all of life.

I. Jesus in the Midst Is the Key to Peacefulness

"Then the same day at evening, being the first day of the week, when the doors were shut where the disciples were assembled for fear of the Jews, came Jesus and stood in the midst, and saith unto them, 'Peace be unto you'" (John 20:19).

When Jesus said "Peace be unto you," He meant more than "May you be safe from trouble." He meant, "May God give you every good thing!"

Isaiah promised, "Thou wilt keep him in perfect peace, whose mind is stayed on thee: because he trusteth in thee" (26:3).

A man had to cross a wide river on the ice. He was afraid it might be too thin, so he began to crawl on his hands and knees in great horror. He feared he might fall through at any moment. Just as he neared the shore, all exhausted, another man glided past him nonchalantly sitting on a sled loaded with pig iron.

How like some Christians! Headed for heaven, they tremble at every step lest the divine promises break under their feet. They only need to listen to the words of Christ as He said to His fearful disciples, "Peace be unto you." Isaiah was right. God will keep those in perfect peace whose minds are stayed on Christ because they trust in Christ (26:3).

Remember that we have peace *with* God through faith in our Lord Jesus Christ according to Romans 5:1. This is the *birthright* of every believer. But we can have the peace *of* God, which passes all understanding. This is the *blessing* of every believer.

Have you ever considered what a blessing it is when occasionally our problems pile up so high we can't possibly solve them? Now don't misunderstand me. I am not saying we are to be delighted about the many troubles that cross our pathways. I am suggesting we should be glad that they are more than we can handle. Why? Because when we finally realize we can't carry the weight of the world on our shoulders, we have taken the first step in overcoming worry and bringing peace into our hearts.

Most of us assume far more responsibility for the future than God ever intended. We are like the fellow who was talking with an acquaintance one day about the hectic nature of the business world. The conversation went something like this: "John, you look worried."

"Man," said the friend, "I've got so many troubles that if anything else happens today that is bad, it will be at least two weeks before I can get around to worrying about it."

Jesus gave some sound advice when He said, "Therefore do not be anxious about tomorrow, for tomorrow will be anxious for itself" (Matt. 6:34). Jesus in the midst is the key to peacefulness. He said, "Peace I leave with you" (John 14:27).

II. Jesus in the Midst Is the Key to Joyfulness

When Jesus walked into the locked upper room where the disciples were meeting, He said, "Peace be unto you"! He showed the disciples His hands and His side. "Then were the disciples glad, when they saw the Lord" (John 20:20). Here is a whole new dimension in the Christian life!

Small wonder these disciples were glad. Jesus had walked into death, entered into Sheol, and emerged again with the keys of death and hell in His belt, having conquered the grave by His resurrection. Reflecting on this tremendous event, John wrote years later: "Ye are of God, little children, and have overcome them [every evil spirit]: because greater is he that is in you, than he that is in the world" (1 John 4:4).

Billy Graham once visited our troops while they were fighting in Korea. Around 5:00 a.m. he was awakened to go to a prayer and praise service. They arrived at the place where the little church was assembled. It was twenty degrees below zero; the bitter wind made it feel still colder. The front and back walls had been blown out of the church. Two side walls remained, with no roof or heat. The people were on their knees praying. Billy Graham could not understand what they saying, so he asked someone to translate. The translator responded, "They are all praying the same prayer: 'Thank you, Jesus!'"

Jesus used the phrase, "Be of good cheer," several times. He spoke of *forgiveness:* "Be of good cheer, thy sins be forgiven thee." He spoke of *companionship:* "Be of good cheer, it is I, be not afraid." And He spoke of *victory:* "Be of good cheer, I have overcome the world."

These expressions cover the whole of life—past, present, and future. The sin of the past is blotted out for the Christian. The continual fellowship of Christ is offered for the present. And the future will reveal Christ as the Conqueror of the world. This is possible because Jesus is in the midst of the believer's life, bringing joy!

III. Jesus in the Midst Is the Key to Usefulness

When Jesus said, "As my Father hath sent me, even so send I you" (John 20:21), He meant that He needs the church. The apostle Paul called the church the body of Christ. The church is to be a mouth to speak for Jesus, feet to run errands for Jesus, hands to do the work of Jesus, and a heart to love for Jesus.

When Jesus said, "As my Father hath sent Me, even so send I you," He meant that the church needs Him. If I had a glove and I said to the glove, "Glove, pick up that Bible," could the glove do it?

The glove has the shape of a hand, with a thumb and fingers. But could the glove pick up a Bible? You respond, "No, it could not." You are quite right. Why? I haven't shown it how.

I say again to the glove, "I apologize, Mr. Glove, I have not told you how to pick up the Bible. Put your thumb on top, the fingers underneath, squeeze tight, and lift." Very simple, isn't it? "That's the way to pick up the Bible, Glove. Now, pick it up."

Will anything happen? No! Why? Because the glove is powerless. It doesn't have what it takes. The glove is empty of life. I could say to the glove again and again, "Pick up the Bible," but the glove could never do it. The glove could never do it until I put my hand into the glove. My hand is what makes the difference.

The moment my hand is it, the glove becomes as strong as my hand. Everything possible for my hand becomes possible for the glove. If the glove could speak, it would say, "I can do all things through the hand which is my strength." You are the glove; Christ is the hand. But there is one difference. When Jesus Christ found you, you were a dirty glove inside and out, so He died to cleanse you. Then through His resurrection He sent the power of the Holy Spirit to indwell you, and now Christ wants to live in that glove—you—the one He has cleansed. Once Christ lives in you, you can say, "I can do all things through Christ which strengtheneth me" (Phil. 4:13).

If you cannot describe the Christian life in any other way, simply say, "Lord Jesus, I am just a glove, and You are the hand." But in order for the glove to be useful, it has to be identified with the hand and available to the hand. If you are going to be used by God, you must be identified with Christ and available to Christ so that He becomes the strength of your life.

Jesus in the midst is the key to usefulness. He said, "As my Father hath sent me, even so send I you."

IV. Jesus in the Midst Is the Key to Powerfulness

"When he had said this, he breathed on them, and saith unto them, Receive ye the Holy Ghost: Whose soever sins ye remit, they are remitted unto them; and whose soever sins ye retain, they are retained" (John 20:22-23).

Jesus breathed on His disciples and gave them the Holy Spirit. There is no doubt that when John wrote this, he was remembering the story of creation. The writer of Genesis says, "The Lord God formed man of the dust of the ground, and breathed into his nostrils the breath of life; and man became a living soul" (Gen. 2:7). The coming of the Holy Spirit is like a new creation. It is like the wakening of life from the dead. When the Holy Spirit comes upon a person, he or she is born again and recreated to do the will of God.

The Greek word *labete* is the word translated as "receive" in John 20:22. It is the second aorist imperative active of *lambanō*, and it means "take," "seize." In other words, when Jesus breathed on His disciples, He said, "Take the Holy Spirit."

There is a natural reluctance on the part of Christians to take this gift of God. We shrink from receiving this priceless possession of God's presence in our lives because we feel unworthy.

Emperor Alexander once ruled all of Russia. On one occasion he presented to one of his lowly servants a rare and expensive golden cup. The poor slave drew back and said, "Your Majesty, it is too much for me to take."

For a moment the Czar hesitated, and then he thrust the chalice into the hand of his servant, replying, "But it is not too much for me to give!"

This is our predicament. We shrink from taking the precious gift of God's Spirit, saying, "I am not worthy; it is too much for me to receive." But our matchless Savior, with His nail-pierced hands, thrusts the gift of the Holy Spirit into our lives, saying, "Take it! Take it! It is not too much for Me to give."

Would you today look up into heaven into the face of your Savior and say: "Oh, blessed Lord Jesus, unworthy though I am, I receive the Holy Spirit. May He fill my life with His presence."

The precious gift of the sweet Holy Spirit is ours forever for the receiving.

Peacefulness, joyfulness, usefulness, and powerfulness are yours. What is the key? Who is the key? Jesus "in the midst"!

3
Working in the Church

(Matt. 3:13-17)

An enthusiastic man said to G. Campbell Morgan, "What the preacher ought to do is catch the spirit of the age in which he is living."

Morgan threw up his hands, exclaiming, "God forgive him if he does! The preacher's job is to correct the spirit of his age."

Uniquely, this was the ministry of John the Baptist. John had a one-stringed instrument and played only one note on that one string. His instrument was his sermon, and the note was the message of repentance. John kept preaching, "Repent ye, for the kingdom of heaven is at hand" (3:2).

By any standard, John was tremendously successful. Judge him by numerical success. He was not the pastor of a large church in a great city; he preached in the wilderness of Judea. Yet the multitudes streamed from the cities and villages to hear his messages. Judge him by results. Never before had anyone demanded that the Jews be baptized. Proselyte Gentiles were baptized upon entering the Jewish faith, but John preached to his own people that they were sinners, needing to repent and be baptized like Gentile proselytes. Judge John by the evaluation of Jesus Christ. Our Lord said, "Among those born of women there has risen no one greater than John the Baptist" (Matt. 11:11).

At the zenith of John's ministry, he encountered Jesus of Nazareth. Christ stepped out of the crowd and said, "John, I want you to baptize Me."

John responded, "Instead of me baptizing You, You ought to baptize me." Jesus responded, "I want you to allow it to be this way because this will fulfill the righteousness of God." John took Jesus into the Jordan River and immersed Him. As Christ came up out of the water, the Spirit of God descended upon Him in the form of a dove. The Heavenly Father said, "This is my beloved Son, in whom I am well pleased" (v. 17).

Here is a tremendous theophany—a manifestation of the triune God. God the Son was baptized. God the Spirit descended upon Christ. God the Father spoke from heaven. The baptism of Jesus was the ordination of our Lord for His ministry. He was endowed with the tools He needed to fulfill His messianic role. This passage teaches how Jesus fulfilled His ministry and tells us how we should work in God's kingdom.

I. The Prevailing Attitude of the Kingdom—Humility

The baptism of Jesus vividly illustrates that humility is the prevailing attitude we must possess as we work in the church. John was baptizing sinners. When Christ was baptized, He ran the risk that someone might think Him to be a sinner in need of repentance. We know that Jesus was sinlessly perfect (2 Cor. 5:21), but He was baptized to fulfill all righteousness, give us an example, and identify Himself with humanity. He knew it to be the will of God.

Notice also the humility of John. John was extremely reluctant to baptize Christ. Indeed, he said that he was not even worthy to unlace Jesus' sandals. Though assertive, successful, gifted, and bold, John was a very humble man.

When John baptized Jesus, what happened? Did Roman trumpets blast? Did angels descend from heaven? No. A bird came from the sky, symbolizing the Holy Spirit. Was the bird a proud Roman eagle? No. It was a humble dove—a dove that would be sacrificed by a poor man when he went to the temple to confess his sins.

The plain teaching of the baptism of Jesus is that as we work for God in the church, we must have the attitude of John and of Jesus—the attitude of humility. Without exception, the people that God uses to do His work are humble and submissive to His will. For example, Moses delivered two million people from bondage, but the Bible says he was the meekest man on the face of the earth (Num. 12:3).

One of the greatest statements about what God requires is found in the Book of Micah, "What doth the Lord require of thee, but to do justly, and to love mercy, and to walk humbly with thy God?" (6:8). As Jesus began His Sermon on the Mount, He said, "Blessed are the poor in spirit: for theirs is the kingdom of heaven" (Matt. 5:3). A free translation would be: "Blessed are those who realize their utter helplessness and who have put their whole trust in God." Those are the individuals God will use—ones characterized by humility.

The word *humility* comes from the Latin word *humus*, which means "ground." A humble person is one who is lowly and does not think himself or herself something he or she really is not. Humility is the golden virtue of the Christian life. It is the most fragile of all virtues, for once we think we have it, we have already lost it.

Humility displaces pride, the root of all sins. Having humility means that we do not get our feelings hurt. The humble person is like the ground—when stepped on, it does not complain. A humble person puts God first, others second, and self last. No task is too lowly for the humble person. Each of us can accomplish a great deal in the kingdom of Christ . . . if we do not care who gets the credit. In the kingdom of Christ, the way to the top is downstairs. Therefore, sink yourself into the highest place!

There is an ancient fable that tells how the angels were impressed by the godly and beautiful life of an aged saint. Coming down from heaven to visit, the angel offered to give the man the gift of miracles. By the touch of his hand, he could heal the sick, restore sight to the blind, and bring the dead back to life. "Oh, no," the saint responded, "the ability to heal belongs to God alone."

The angel suggested, "Then let me give you the ability to bring people under conviction so that the unsaved will come to God."

"No, that's not for me either. That ability belongs only to God the Holy Spirit."

"Then at least," the angel offered, "you can let me make you the very person of virtue so people will be drawn to you by the virtue of your life."

The aged man responded, "No, God forbid! Jesus Christ alone is our example. If people were drawn to me, they might not be drawn to Him."

"Then what gift do you desire?"

The saint responded, "Only this: that I might have His grace, so that I might do good to all men without their knowing that I did it." With this attitude, we can accomplish a great deal for God's glory as we serve Him through the church.

II. The Dynamic of the Kingdom—Holy Spirit Power

The Bible teaches that Jesus was the only begotten Son of God, conceived by the Holy Spirit. When Jesus was baptized in the Jordan River, the Spirit of God descended upon Him in the form of a dove. Jesus Himself later said, "The Spirit of the Lord is upon me, because he hath anointed me" (Luke 4:18). Indeed, no mighty work for God has ever been done apart from the endowment, the enablement of the Holy Spirit.

Elijah was a great prophet. Elisha, his student said, "Let me do the works that you do. Give me a double portion of your spirit."

Elijah responded, "It is not for me to give; but if when I go into heaven you see me depart, you'll know that your request has been granted." The two prophets talked on, and "behold, there appeared a chariot of fire, and horses of fire, and parted them both asunder; and Elijah went up by a whirlwind into heaven. And Elisha saw it, and he cried, My father, my father, the chariot of Israel, and the horsemen thereof" (2 Kings 2:11-12). Thus the mantle of Elijah fell upon Elisha, and he did even greater works than his prophet teacher.

So it is true of your life and mine. If the mantle of the Holy Spirit clothes us and if we are filled with His presence, we then can do mighty works to glorify the name of God. The disciples were Christians before Pentecost, but the Bible states that at Pentecost they were all filled with the Holy Spirit. From this milestone the church moved out into worldwide evangelism. The disciples could not have won the world to Christ by staying in the upper room, neither could they have won anyone to Christ without waiting in the upper room.

When Saul of Tarsus was converted, Ananias came to him and said, "Brother Saul, the Lord, even Jesus . . . hath sent me, [that I might touch your eyes and] thou mightest receive thy sight, and be filled with the Holy [Spirit]" (Acts 9:17). This is the pressing need we have as born-again believers. We need that divine infilling to empower us to do God's work. There is no substitute for Holy Spirit power.

The church has been guilty of using many substitutes for the Holy Spirit. We have tried *activism*. We have told people that they ought to *do* something, while the Bible says they ought to *be* something. One can be as busy as a bee and have just about as much spiritual power. We have tried *aesthetics*, making beauty a ritual. Sometimes we feel that if we can make our churches beautiful, then people will automatically be drawn to God. We may have all of the colors in the rainbow in our stained glass windows, but they cannot cover the blackness of sin in a person's heart. We need God's Spirit in our lives.

Another substitute for the Holy Spirit is *organization*. Remember that organization in itself never produces power. Organization is only a channel through which power flows. A Cadillac automobile without gas will not go as far as a spasmodic mule with a mouth full of corn. The Cadillac may be better organized, but it lacks the power. We need more than organization. We need the power of the living God.

Another substitute for Holy Spirit power is *intellectualism*. There is nothing wrong with knowledge. The apostle Paul said that knowledge is good if it edifies. It is true, however, that the cold winds of intellectualism often stifle the fires of evangelism. I respect great students and scholars. We need what they do and accomplish, but we also need the Spirit of the living God.

When Bishop Simpson preached years ago in Memorial Hall in London, he preached quietly and with little gesticulation but with great power. A young professor and one of his students came to critique Bishop Simpson's speech. Though he sat with pencil and paper in hand, the professor never made a note during the entire sermon. Afterward the student asked, "How did you like the speech of Bishop Simpson? What did you think of his homiletics, his organization, his elocution?"

The professor confessed, "I don't know anything about his homiletics, his organization, or his elocution. All I know is that Bishop Simpson has the power of the living God."

That is what we need in our lives. That was the secret of the attracting power of Jesus Christ. And that was the secret of the success of the first-century church. The dynamic of the kingdom is Holy Spirit power.

III. The Objective of the Kingdom—Redemption

The baptism of Jesus reveals that the prevailing attitude of the kingdom of God is humility, the dynamic of the kingdom is Holy Spirit power, and the objective of the kingdom is redemption.

We can see that objective symbolized in the baptism of Jesus. The Bible tells us that when Jesus was baptized in the Jordan River, the Spirit of God descended upon Him like a dove. God spoke and said, "This is my beloved Son, in whom I am well pleased" (v. 17). In the baptism of Jesus, God was saying in three ways that the object of the ministry of His Son was to win people to salvation and life everlasting.

A. Baptism

First, what does baptism symbolize? It symbolizes that Jesus was buried and was raised from the grave (Rom. 6:4). So when Jesus was baptized, He was pointing toward His death and saying, "I'm going to die to redeem humankind."

B. The Dove

Second, the Bible says that when Jesus was baptized, a dove came out of heaven. The dove was the little bird offered by a poor man in the temple so that his sin could be cleansed and forgiven. The baptism of Jesus was stating that through the death of Christ people can be forgiven of sin.

C. God's Voice

Third, when Jesus was baptized, God spoke and said, "This is my beloved Son, in whom I am well pleased." That sentence is composed of two quotations from the Old Testament. "This is my beloved Son" is taken from Psalm 2:7. That psalm is a description of the Messiah. So when God spoke at Jesus' baptism, He revealed from heaven that Jesus was to be the Messiah: "This is my beloved Son"; Jesus is the Christ. "In whom I am well pleased" is taken from Isaiah 42:1, which is a description of the Suffering Servant. In that statement, God revealed that as the Messiah, Jesus would die for His people—His throne would be a cross.

As workers in the kingdom of God, we need to know the objective of the kingdom. The objective is to win people to Christ and to help them to grow in discipleship—the objective is redemption. Jesus summarized His entire ministry in one sentence, "For the Son of man is come to seek and to save that which was lost" (Luke 19:10).

Teacher, are you teaching to win your students to Christ? Choir member, are you singing to bring people to a saving knowledge of Christ? Usher, are you ushering people into church so that they might be saved by the grace of God? Are we witnessing so that lost souls can be saved? We must, because the object of the kingdom is redemption.

Years ago, an hermit lived in the mountains of Virginia. The village boys laughed at the old man. One of them decided to play a trick. He said to his friend, "I know how we can fool him. I'll take a live bird, hold it in my hand, and ask him what it is. When he answers, I'll then ask whether it's alive or dead. If he says it's dead, I'll let it fly away. If he says it's alive, I'll crush it."

The boys trapped a bird, then found the old hermit at the door of his house. "I have a question for you. What is it I hold in my hand?"

"Well, my son, it looks like a sparrow you've caught."

"Right, then tell me, Is it alive or dead?"

The old man knew their intention. He fixed his eyes on the boy for a long moment. Then he said, "It is as you will, my son."

How goes the work of your church? It is as you will! But characterized by humility, energized by the power of the Holy Spirit, and with redemption as our goal, we cannot fail!

4
The Lord's Supper

(1 Cor. 11:23-26)

The geographical heart of London is Charing Cross. All distances are measured from it. This spot is referred to simply as "the Cross." A lost child was one day picked up by a London bobby. The child was unable to tell where he lived. Finally, in response to the repeated questions of the policeman, and amid his sobs and tears, the little fellow said, "If you'll take me to the cross, I think I can find my way from there."

The cross of Jesus Christ is the point where we become reconciled to God. If we find our way to God and home to heaven, we must first come to the cross of the Lord Jesus Christ. It is important for Christians to participate regularly in observing the Lord's Supper because it takes us to the cross.

On that fateful night before Christ was crucified, He met with His disciples in the upper room in Jerusalem. They observed the Passover together. As they were eating, Jesus took bread, blessed it, broke it, and gave it to the disciples, saying: "Take, eat; this is my body" (Matt. 26:26).

Jesus then took the cup, and when He had given thanks, He gave it to the disciples, saying, "Drink ye all of it" (Matt. 26:27). Our Lord went on to explain that the bread represented His body, which would be given for them on the cross, and that the wine represented His blood of the New Testament, which would be shed for the forgiveness of their sins (Matt. 26:28).

Since that fateful night nearly two thousand years ago, Christians have come to the supper of the Lord to worship Christ, fellowship with God, and solemnly remind themselves of the price that Jesus Christ paid for their redemption.

I. The Lord's Supper Is a Divine Command

The celebration of the Lord's Supper is a divine command for every one of God's children. When our Savior instituted the Lord's Supper, He said, "This is my body which is given for you: this do in remembrance of me" (Luke 22:19). The Lord's Supper, then, is a solemn obligation that rests upon every Christian.

Every child of God is obligated to assemble with the people of God for the celebration of the memorial of Christ's death at the Lord's Supper. To neglect to do so is to be disobedient to the Lord's direct command. Jesus said, "This do"! Every Christian is commanded to observe the death of Christ at the Lord's Supper.

The same Bible that tells us not to steal, not to kill, not to commit adultery, not to bear false witness, and not to covet, also commands us to observe the Lord's Supper. If it is a sin to murder, to steal, to lie, or to bear false witness, it is also a sin not to take the Lord's Supper. It is a sin of omission.

The Lord's table is like a great bridge, spanning the church's history on earth. One end rests on the shame of the cross, the other is planted in the glory of the kingdom. This meal sustains a threefold relationship to the Christian. It is the reminder of our past justification. It is the source of our present sustenance in the new life. It is the pledge of our future blessedness and glory.

In 1 Corinthians 11 Paul tells us that the Lord's Supper is a table of remembrance (v. 24). He goes on to relate that it is a table of obedience: "Take, eat; . . . Drink ye all of it" (Matt. 26:26-27). It should be a table of self-examination (v. 28). It is surely a table of communion. (1 Cor. 10:16). The Lord's Supper helps us to worship God and becomes a table of thanksgiving (11:24). It helps us to search our hearts and becomes a table of confession (v. 26). Gloriously, the Lord's Supper is a table of expectation because we are to observe it "till he come" (v. 26).

II. The Lord's Supper Is a Blessed Privilege

More than a divine command, the Lord's Supper is a blessed privilege. We ought to welcome every opportunity to come to the Lord's table because of the great privilege the Lord bestows in permitting us to worship Him. This is the table *of the Lord*. Think of that. It is not the table of an assembly or a church or a communion but the table of the Lord. He is the Host. He is the Master of the house. We poor, stumbling, faltering creatures are invited to come and sit at His table. What a privilege!

A godly old country pastor was in the midst of his Communion service, and, suddenly, his quick eye detected a woman passing the cup untasted. She sat among the people quietly weeping. At once his kindly heart sensed the situation. Who of us has not at such time been so conscious of our own unworthiness and sinfulness as to shrink from partaking of that blessed cup?

The loving pastor knew the gospel of Christ too well to let one of his parishioners suffer thus. He hastened down the aisle. He took the cup from the hands of the serving deacon, and stepping up to the weeping woman, he pressed it into her hand with the loving, tender exhortation, "Take it, take it. It's for sinners; it's for sinners!"

III. The Lord's Supper Is a Necessary Memorial

You and I should regularly partake of the Lord's Supper because it reminds us of the cost of our salvation. It is a necessary memorial given to us to remind us of the price that Jesus Christ paid that you and I might be forgiven of our sin.

The Lord said, "This do . . . in remembrance of me." Jesus was inferring that the Lord's people, after all that He has done, may forget the great price that has been paid for their redemption. The God who knows our heart better than any of us knows that we are yet so human and wayward that if He did not constantly remind us, we would soon, too soon, forget. How often during the week do you think about the price that Jesus paid for your redemption? So the Lord tenderly rebukes us in this supper and says: "You tend to become thankless, and if I do not provide a reminder, you would all too soon forget what it cost Me to purchase your salvation."

The Lord's Supper is given to keep our love aflame and our hearts aglow for Jesus. Jesus gave us the Lord's Supper to remind us that we are but dust and that even though redeemed, we might forget the death of Christ on the cross of Calvary. The Lord's Supper reminds us that it is God's faithfulness that saves us and not our own. If God had forgotten us as often as we forget Him, there would be no hope for our redemption.

Jesus used two elements in the Lord's Supper: bread and wine. The bread symbolizes the body of our Lord. Though the Scripture teaches that not a *bone* of Christ's body was broken, His *body* was broken on the cross of Calvary. The spikes pierced His hands and feet, the spear pierced His body and opened His heart. Jesus' body was broken and sacrificed for us on the cross.

The fruit of the vine reminds us of the shed blood of our Savior. The Bible teaches that without the shedding of blood there is no remission of sin. When we partake of the Lord's Supper, we publicly state that our redemption was purchased at the tremendous price of the shed blood of Jesus Christ. We are not redeemed by corruptible things, such as silver and gold, but by the precious blood of Christ (1 Pet. 1:18).

A lady was lying dangerously ill. A clergyman had been sent for, and he gave her Communion. It failed to give her peace. After the minister left, the sufferer turned to the occupant of the bed nearest her own and said sadly, "I thought it would have done me more good." The other, an earnest Christian lady, quickly replied, "Ah, you don't want it; you want *Him!*" This is why we observe the Lord's Supper. It is a necessary memorial to remind us of Him who loved us and gave Himself for us.

IV. The Lord's Supper Is a Willing Testimony

Years ago, when I pastored a wonderful country church, we would often have testimony meetings on Sunday evening. One by one, members of the congregation would stand and testify regarding their love for Jesus Christ. Across the years, I have remembered those testimony meetings with great joy, and they have continued to be a source of encouragement to my life spiritually. In like manner, when we come to partake of the Lord's Supper, we are giving a testimony regarding our faith in Jesus Christ. Paul wrote: "For as often as ye eat this bread and drink this cup, ye do shew the Lord's death" (1 Cor. 11:26). Every time we come together to break bread and drink of the cup, we are testifying that we have experienced in our lives the benefits of Christ's death and cleansing power. We witness to the fact that we are saved and have appropriated by faith the finished work of the Lord Jesus on our behalf when He died on the cruel cross of Calvary.

When I take the bread of the Lord's Supper, I testify by that act that I believe that Christ's body was broken for me at Calvary. When I drink of the cup at the Lord's Supper, I am testifying that I believe that His blood was shed that my sins might be cleansed. The Lord's Supper is a willing testimony of our faith in Christ.

V. The Lord's Supper Is a Humbling Confession

Have you ever stopped to consider that by taking the elements of the Lord's Supper you are confessing that your sins are so great, and your iniquities are so vile, that it took nothing less than the death of Christ, the Son of God, and the shedding of His precious blood to set you free from your sin? Away go all excuses and away go all good works when we partake of the Lord's Supper. Here we confess that we are not only sinners, but great sinners. We confess that we were so utterly and hopelessly lost in sin that nothing in heaven or on earth could pay the price of our redemption except the infinite sacrifice of the precious Son of God sent from heaven.

The death of Christ is the death of all human righteousness. By observing the Lord's Supper, I therefore acknowledge myself to be totally and completely unfit in myself. I am renouncing all of my human goodness, and I am confessing, as I take the Lord's Supper, that "My hope is built on nothing less/Than Jesus' blood and righteousness."

VI. The Lord's Supper Is an Act of Faith

While the Lord's Supper looks back to the cross, it looks forward to the crown as well. Paul told the Corinthians to continue to partake of the Lord's Supper until Jesus comes again.

Remember that the church is the bride of Christ. When Jesus comes again, He will take his bride to heaven, and the marriage supper of the Lamb will occur. In heaven we will not need the Lord's Supper, for we will be with the Lord!

The Lord's Supper is from coming to coming. It is from the first coming of Christ until His second coming. It is a memorial only for the time of Jesus' absence. The Lord's Supper is an act of faith on the part of the church to testify that Christ has come and died for our sins on the cross. It anticipates the day when He will come again to take us home to heaven to the crown. The Lord's Supper looks forward to the blessed second coming of Jesus Christ.

A speaker, in commenting on the words of the institution of the Lord's Supper, "This do . . . in remembrance of me," called attention to the fact that here there is a "great absence." We are to recall Christ's former presence and await His coming. You and I are to partake of the Lord's Supper until He comes or until we go to meet Him as He takes us home to heaven through the door of death.

5
The Amazing Church

(Acts 2:1-12)

What an amazing service they had on the Day of Pentecost! One hundred and twenty disciples had been praying and waiting ten days. Suddenly there was a sound like a cyclone. It was a mighty, rushing wind. Every believer was filled with God's Spirit. Resting upon each of them was a cloven tongue like a fire. They looked like human candles!

Then a marvelous miracle took place. As these disciples witnessed in their native Galilean tongue, those present heard their own language. Something exciting was happening! Three thousand people became Christians that day.

Luke recorded that the people present "were all amazed and marvelled" (Acts 2:7). Two questions began to be asked by the unbelievers. The first was, "What meaneth this?" (Acts 2:12) The second question recorded in Acts 2:37 is the result of the first question. Pierced in their hearts, they said to Peter, "What shall we do?" These people wanted their hearts made right with God. They wanted to be saved and be certain they were going to heaven.

Today's church has been trying to get the unsaved to ask the second question "What shall we do?" before they ask the first question: "What meaneth this?" We have been trying to get the unchurched to want what we have without first being amazed at what we are. We are trying to get them saved and into the church, but we have not shown them anything different in our lives.

It is a tragedy that the unsaved people coming to church often are not amazed. They do not wonder, nor are they perplexed. They do not see anything different in the average church today. They are not asking, "What does this mean?" and then, following that with the question, "What must we do to be saved?"

I believe our Lord wants the church today to be like that first-century church at Pentecost. Billy Graham preached a crusade in a certain city. Often in his sermons, Graham states: "The Bible says." One man remarked, "Billy Graham is going to set evangelism back fifty years." When Graham heard that, he responded, "Oh, I did not mean to do that. I don't want to set evangelism back fifty years. I want to set evangelism back 2,000 years."

That is exactly what we need to do. We need to move back to the first-century church at Jerusalem on the Day of Pentecost and do what they did. If we prayed as they prayed, believed as they believed, witnessed as they witnessed, evidenced enthusiasm as they were enthusiastic, were filled with the Spirit as they were filled, we can achieve what they achieved.

There are three reasons we can do as those first-century Christians did. First, our God is the same. God has not changed. He still loves the lost. His mercy, grace, goodness, and love abound. He is still seeking the unsaved. He still is not willing that any should perish but that all should come to repentance.

Do you remember a few years ago when they were telling us that God was dead? Aren't you glad that the "God is dead" movement is dead! I like what one wonderful black minister said. "They are talking about how God is dead. Of course, God isn't dead! In the first place, you have to know the deceased well enough to identify the corpse. These reporting God is dead do not know Him."

"In the second place, when a death occurs, they always notify the next of kin. I am a son. Nobody has notified me."

Then the minister said, "In the third place, what if God did die? Why, all He would do is resurrect Himself and start over again!"

No, God is not dead. He is alive and well! But some of us act as if God were sick. There was a time that God could rescue the perishing, care for the dying, and snatch them in pity from the sin and the grave. But, we act like God cannot do that any more.

God is just as powerful this moment as He has ever been. It is an insult to God to say we cannot have revival and a harvest of the unsaved today. We can have Pentecostal power today because God has not changed. How could God change? He is God!

Second, not only is our Master the same, but humankind is the same. Humanity has not really changed. I hear people say, "Today men are more wicked than they used to be." I disagree because Adam and Eve were totally depraved. One can't get any worse than that. Cain, their first son, was a murderer. He killed his own brother, Abel.

People have always been wicked. God has never had good people to work with. Don't think that in the first century there were suddenly an unusual number of nice people, and God took these nice people and did something wonderful with them. The people in the first century nailed Jesus to the cross. Yet, in the first century the church ministered with great power, and souls were saved.

Third, our methods should not change. God has given us the message of the gospel and the blueprint for success in the Great Commission. Our Master has not changed, humankind has not changed, and our methods should not change. God teaches us in Acts 2 what the church ought to do. I believe that God has a well-defined plan for what the church is to do. What is God's method, blueprint, plan, and design for the amazing church?

I. The Right Atmosphere in the Church

The golden characteristic of the New Testament church was unity, oneness, and accord. Luke stated: "When the day of Pentecost was fully come, they were all with one accord in one place" (Acts 2:1). These people were not rusted together by tradition, nor wired together by organization, nor frozen together by formalism. They were melted together by a common Spirit, the Holy Spirit, the Spirit of love.

"Blessed are the peacemakers: for they shall be called the children of God" taught Jesus in Matthew 5:9. According to the writer of Proverbs, among the six things that God hates is someone who sows discord among the brethren (Prov. 6:19). How good it is for brethren to dwell together in unity.

Some said concerning the first-century Christians, "Behold, how they love one another." Jesus said, "By this shall all men know that ye are my disciples, if ye have love one to another" (John 13:35). We may have differences; but, if we are to do what Christ wants us to do, we must bury these differences between ourselves and love one another, saying, "Jesus is Lord." There are not enough demons in hell to stop a church bonded together in love.

Small wonder that the world was amazed at the first-century church. The believers were assembled together, and they were in accord. This church had the right atmosphere. It was a spiritual atmosphere!

II. The Right Appeal from the Church

The amazing first-century church was led by Almighty God to make the right appeal to the unsaved. This is a threefold process. First, there is the anointing of the Holy Spirit. Second, there is the action of personal witnessing. Third, there is the authority of the Word of God.

A. Anointing

These first-century Christians were all filled with the Holy Spirit (Acts 2:4). The work of God can only be done through the power of the Holy Spirit. It is every believer's privilege and responsibility to be filled with the Holy Spirit (Eph. 5:18).

It was not just the preacher that was filled with the Holy Spirit at Pentecost. Peter told the audience that the promise was unto them, their children, their sons, their daughters, and as many as the Lord our God shall call (Acts 2:17-18).

At Pentecost, the Bible says there was a sound like a cyclone, then there appeared cloven tongues as of fire. Following that, as the Christians opened their mouths in praise and witnessing, the speech that came out was not in their own language but in various foreign languages. You and I do not need to repeat the miracle of Pentecost any more than we need to repeat the virgin birth of Christ or the vicarious death of Christ. Pentecost was a once-and-for-all event. We cannot repeat it, but we surely can experience the same power today, just as we celebrate the birth of our Lord and rejoice that He died to cleanse us of our sins.

God was *with us* when Jesus Christ was born and placed in the cradle at Bethlehem. Supernatural events surrounded Bethlehem. There was the new star in the heavens. There was the virgin birth. There was the angelic chorus, and when Jesus was born, He was given the name *Emmanuel,* which interpreted means "God with us." None of these miracles need to be repeated, but aren't you glad for Bethlehem?

At Calvary we are taught that God is *for us.* The Bible says that Christ died for our sins according to the Scriptures (1 Cor. 15:1-4). He died once and for all. Aren't you glad there's not going to be another Calvary? Wouldn't it be a terrible thing if every time the church were to come together, we would say, "We are going to repeat Calvary. We are going to crucify Jesus again." That would be most blasphemous.

At Calvary a number of miracles took place. There was the earthquake, the darkness, the graves were opened, and the souls and bodies of saints came out of the graves. We cannot repeat that. We do not want to repeat that, but we surely can be blessed by it.

B. Action

When the Day of Pentecost began, there were 120 dedicated Christians in an upper room praying. When the day ended, 3,000 new converts had been added to the congregation. How did this occur? The Bible tells us in Acts 1:14 that the disciples prayed. Their prayer was followed by witnessing. In Acts 2:4, we read: "They were all filled with the Holy Ghost, and began to speak with other tongues, as the Spirit gave them utterance." These were not angelic languages. The Jewish Christians spoke in their native Galilean tongue (Acts 2:7). The Holy Spirit performed a miracle, and the people present heard the message of salvation in their own language (Acts 2:8).

When there was a question about the miracle that had taken place, Simon Peter began to share his witness. He related to them how Joel had prophesied that God would send the Holy Spirit (Acts 2:15-21). He then told them how the works of Jesus proved He is the anointed Messiah sent from heaven prophesied by King David (Acts 2:22-31). Finally, Peter said the resurrection of Jesus Christ proves He is both Lord and Christ (Acts 2:32-36).

Here Christ's church makes the right appeal to the unsaved. It is an appeal anointed by the Holy Spirit and put into positive action by the witnessing of the people and the preacher. The results were miraculous. We too can witness miraculous results anointed by the Holy Spirit. We need to put our faith into action by sharing God's message of redemption through faith in Jesus Christ.

C. Authority

When the anointing power of the Holy Spirit was called into question by the people at Pentecost, Peter appealed to the authority of the Word of God. The Bible indicates that some of the people present that day mocked the church (Acts 2:13). Their mocking was turned to repentance when Peter quoted the prophet Joel (Acts 2:17-21). Peter also quoted Psalm 16:8-11, written by David, and beautifully related this psalm to the resurrection of Jesus Christ from the dead.

The Bible tells us that "faith cometh by hearing, and hearing by the word of God" (Rom. 10:17). The sword of the Spirit is the Word of God. This is the weapon that God uses to free men and women, boys and girls from the shackles of sin. The right appeal from the church is always based on the authority of the Word of God.

III. The Right Attitude from the Lost

When the right atmosphere exists in the church and the right appeal is made from the church, the unsaved usually respond with the right attitude. On the Day of Pentecost, the hearts of the unsaved were stirred. They asked Peter and the rest of the apostles, "What shall we do?" Peter's response was that they needed to turn from their sins and to give evidence that their sins had been forgiven by following Jesus in New Testament baptism. He went on to promise them that they would receive the gift of the Holy Spirit (Acts 2:37-38).

When Jesus gave the Great Commission, He said that we are to make disciples, baptize them, and teach them to observe all things that He has commanded (Matt. 28:19-20). At Pentecost, the disciples carried out the Great Commission, for Luke recorded, "Then they that gladly received his word were baptized: and the same day there were added unto them about three thousand souls. And they continued steadfastly in the apostles' doctrine and fellowship, and in breaking of bread, and in prayers" (Acts 2:41-42).

Here is the amazing first-century church carrying out the Great Commission of our Lord.

6
Beyond Conversion

(Acts 2:36-47)

The most wonderful thing that can happen to any individual is for that person to become a Christian. What does God want us to do after we become Christians? In Acts 2, the apostle Peter preached repentance from sin and faith in Jesus Christ as Savior. Then he said, "Save yourselves from this untoward generation" (Acts 2:40)). Peter was saying there is something beyond conversion. The Bible teaches the church what we are to do after we are saved.

I. Beyond Conversion There Is Baptism

In the first century, when people received the Word of God, they were baptized (Acts 2:41). Why were they baptized, and why are we to be baptized?

A Christian is someone who is Christlike. When we are baptized, we are following Jesus' example. Jesus was baptized by John the Baptist in the Jordan River. From Nazareth to the Jordan where John was baptizing was a distance of forty miles. Jesus walked that distance to be baptized by John because He felt it to be so important.

We want to be baptized because this is a direct command of Jesus. In Matthew 28 when Jesus gave the Great Commission, He told us to make disciples, "baptizing them in the name of the Father, and of the Son, and the Holy Ghost." One cannot be obedient to Christ if he or she has not followed Jesus in believer's baptism.

Furthermore, baptism is an expression that we believe that Jesus was buried and resurrected. In Romans 6, Paul tells us that we are buried with Christ in baptism, that like as Christ was raised up from the dead, even so we should walk in newness of life following Him.

At conversion we died to the old sin life, and our sins were cleansed by the blood of Christ. We now have a new life—a resurrected life. Baptism is a picture of that resurrection.

When Jesus was baptized in the Jordan River, He identified Himself with humanity. When we are baptized, we identify ourselves with Christ. When a young man joins the army, he receives a uniform. When a person joins the Christian army, he or she is to wear the uniform of Christ, which is baptism.

Baptism does not save. It is a testimony that we have been saved. Baptism is not essential to salvation, but it is surely essential to obedience.

II. Beyond Conversion There Is Church Membership

When you are converted, you should follow Jesus Christ in believer's baptism. At that point, you become a member of a local church. The Bible teaches that on the Day of Pentecost the Christians were baptized, and they were added to them. What does that mean? It means that they became members of the church. "Then they that gladly received his word were baptized: and the same day there were added unto them about three thousand souls" (Acts 2:41).

I believe in the church because the Bible says that Jesus loved the church and gave Himself for it. As a Christian, I intend to love the church and give myself to it. The Bible exhorts us, "Not forsaking the assembling of ourselves together, as the manner of some is; but exhorting one another: and so much the more, as ye see the day approaching" (Heb. 10:25). Why would the Bible so strongly exhort us to be active in the church?

The church reminds us to worship God. Most of us are so caught up in the affairs of life that we seldom pause to acknowledge our faith in Jesus Christ and our love for Almighty God. The church helps us to do this.

I never will forget the first time I visited Lucerne, Switzerland. We made a breathtaking journey up to the top of Mount Pilatus. Below, I could see the beautiful little city of Lucerne, the lovely river that flowed through it, the meadows with the cows grazing, and over on another hill a small church. Occasionally, the clouds would float by.

From above the city, things below looked different. Worship is like that. It is climbing into God's presence and looking at life from above. It is getting life back into perspective. It is possible to worship God anywhere and anytime, but I have observed that we most often worship God in church.

Someone has said that religion is more often caught than taught. When you and I are with other Christians in church, we have our faith strengthened. The Bible exhorts us, "Let us hold fast the profession of our faith without wavering" (Heb. 10:23). When a person receives Christ as Savior, he or she makes a profession of faith. The writer of Hebrews tells us that we need to hang on to that profession of faith. Worship at church helps us to hold fast and to hang on to our faith.

III. Beyond Conversion There Is Continuing Steadfastly

Jesus admonished His church to be faithful unto death with the promise that He will give us the crown of life (Rev. 2:10). That's exactly what the early church did. "They continued steadfastly in the apostles' doctrine and fellowship, and in breaking of bread, and in prayers" (Acts 2:42).

Only steadfast determination will enable you to reach your full potential in the Christian life. Physical growth may occur naturally, but if we are to grow in grace, it must be supernaturally.

A renowned mountain climber was recounting the ascent of his group in the Alps. Two of the party were lost. The mountain climber reported, "When last seen, the two men were ascending the heights." This should be the approach of every Christian as we continue steadfastly serving Jesus Christ.

Luke recorded that the early Christians continued steadfastly in the apostles' doctrine. This would be the teaching that they had received from their Savior, the Lord Jesus Christ. We have this teaching in written form in the New Testament. You and I are responsible to read the Bible, study the Bible, analyze the Bible, memorize the Bible, and meditate on the Bible.

The Bible is spiritual nourishment for the Christian. It is referred to as bread, honey, milk, and strong meat. A faithful minister was visiting every family in the congregation. Sitting in the living room, he was conversing with the husband and wife when the mother said to her five-year-old son, "Go get our favorite Book." Obediently, the chill returned with the Sears catalog. Is the Bible your favorite Book?

The early church was a fellowshiping church. Someone has said that there is no ship like the good ship *Fellowship*. Church is where you and I can encourage one another.

Again and again as a minister, I have had members remark to me following the death of a loved one, a family crisis, or a long stay in the hospital, "Pastor, I don't know what I would have done without the church." Fellowship is not just having cookies and punch on Sunday night after the worship service. Fellowship is helping one another in adversity, praying for one another in difficulty, putting our arms around one another in sorrow, and sharing with one another the burdens and joys of life.

We are also to continue steadfastly in prayer. In its simplest form prayer is talking to God. Prayer was a vital element in the life of our Lord. Jesus prayed when He was baptized. He prayed all night before He selected His disciples. He prayed at the grave of Lazarus. Before He broke the bread and fed the five thousand, Jesus offered a prayer of thanks. In Gethsemane's garden He prayed, "Not my will, but thine, be done" (Matt. 22:42). When Christ was crucified, He prayed that the Heavenly Father would forgive those who took part in the crucifixion. And in His closing moments on the cross He prayed, "Father into thy hands I commend my spirit." Jesus considers prayer so important that He is spending all of His time between His ascension and second coming as our High Priest. You and I should be like Christ and pray often and earnestly.

Alfred Lord Tennyson said, "More things are wrought by prayer/ Than this world dreams of." And Martin Luther wrote, "Prayer is a powerful thing, for God hath linked himself thereto." Make prayer the habit of your life. Be like the psalmist who wrote, "Seven times a day do I praise thee" (Ps. 119:164).

There are many ways to pray, but perhaps the best is to pray on our knees. Paul taught us to "Pray without ceasing" (1 Thess. 5:17). As we go along through life, everything should remind us to pray.

When you see a flag, pray for your country. When you see a church, pray for the work of God and our missionaries. When you pass by a funeral home, pray for the sorrowing. When you see a school, pray for the children. One motivational speaker said that we spend twenty-seven hours a year at stop lights. If you would pray every time you miss a green light, you would spend twenty-seven more hours each year in fellowship with God.

IV. Beyond Conversion There Is Giving

In the early church, the disciples used their possessions to help one another. The Bible says that they "had all things common" (Acts 2:44). This is not communism. It simply means that they were willing to help one another. It was not government control; it was an individual decision.

The generosity of the early Christians is recorded in Acts 2:45 which tells us that they sold their possessions and distributed them to each other according to the needs of each individual.

One principle that the Bible emphasizes is that of sowing and reaping. God promises us that we are going to reap what we sow, more than we sow, and later than we sow. I believe that this principle applies to giving.

The apostle Paul wrote, "But this I say, He which soweth sparingly shall reap also sparingly; and he which soweth bountifully shall reap also bountifully" (2 Cor. 9:6). If we cast our bread on the waters, it will surely return to us. Paul was teaching the Corinthians that if they wanted God to bountifully bless them, then they should bountifully bless people. The principle is: sow sparingly and reap sparingly—sow bountifully and reap bountifully.

This is a principle that runs all through life. How does a person get more energy? The answer is by using or giving more energy. How does a person get friends? By being friendly. How do you get people to smile at you? You smile at them. How do you get people to love you? You love them. Whatever you put out, that is what you are going to get back. The same is true in our giving to the Lord's work through the church. If we will give our tithes and our offerings liberally, graciously, and joyfully, God promises that this kind of giving will not go unrewarded. Indeed, He promises to open the windows of heaven and pour us out a blessing that there is not room enough to receive (Mal. 3:9-10).

V. Beyond Conversion There Is Gladness and Praise

The Gospel record tells us how one day Jesus asked a rich young ruler to follow Him. Making the wrong decision, the young man turned away from Jesus. The Gospel writer was careful to tell us that he "went away sorrowful" (Matt. 19:22). On the other hand, Luke told us of the conversion of a tax collector by the name of Zacchaeus. When Zacchaeus accepted Jesus Christ as the Lord of His life, the Bible says that he "received him joyfully" (Luke 19:6).

Jesus wants His followers to be joyful. That was the condition of the early church beyond conversion. They were "praising God, and having favour with all the people" (Acts 2:47).

The result of the spiritual condition of the early church was such that "the Lord added to the church daily such as should be saved" (Acts 2:47).

7
The Power of a Praying Church

(Acts 4:23-31)

Acts 4 is an account of a church at prayer. What wonderful things happened! An earthquake shook the building. Christians were filled with the Holy Spirit. Boldly they began to witness. There was unity in the church. The church had great power, and grace was upon every member of the congregation.

Have you ever seen God's power released in and through a church—a local assembly of His people? If so, that church must have been a praying church, for the power of God operates through a praying church. We can pray, believe, and receive, or we can pray, doubt, and do without.

There is a church in Seoul, Korea, that has been marvelously blessed of God. The pastor teaches the people to do two things: pray and witness. They are short in every other area, but they are long in prayer and witnessing. What is the result? The church has nearly 500,000 members. The first Sunday service begins at 6:30 a.m., and the last service begins at 12:00 midnight. The sanctuary seats over 17,000 people. In every worship service there is standing room only. Often the members are asked not to attend the following Sunday so visitors can come and be saved. That is the power of a praying church! That is the pattern of the New Testament church in the Book of Acts.

It's time for the church to have a new emphasis and a new entering into the spirit of corporate prayer. Just as individuals are to pray, the church is to pray as a body.

Problems have always faced Christ's church:
• getting the gospel to the outsider;

- securing spiritual results from our ministry;
- finding the right leaders for the various activities of our church;
- finances;
- the lack of love and unity;
- discipling new converts; and
- some people failing to be submissive and giving themselves to spiritual authority and leadership.

But these are not the critical issues. The real problem is the prayer life of the church. If that problem is solved, every other problem will find a solution. Difficulties will soon disappear; obstacles will be removed when the prayer life of the church is powerful and effective. A praying church quickly becomes a revived church, a worshiping church, a soul-winning church, a giving church, and a spiritual church.

There is only one real problem in every church, and that is to get the members of that church together on their knees before Almighty God.

Luke recorded: "When they had prayed, the place was shaken where they were assembled together; and they were all filled with the Holy Ghost, and they spake the word of God with boldness" (Acts 4:31). So the church needs more than anything else to be a praying church. What are the marks of a praying church? The answer is found in Acts 4:23-31.

I. In a Praying Church There Is a Continuous Desire to Pray

A praying church recognizes the supreme importance of prayer, and always desires to pray. This is illustrated in the lives of the leaders of the Jerusalem church. Peter and John went up to the temple to pray. Later Peter and John were in prison, and while they were there the church prayed. When Peter and John were set free from prison, they immediately hastened to join the church meeting to let them know what happened to them (Acts 4:23).

When the Christians heard their report, what did they do? "They heard . . . they lifted up their voice to God with one accord" (Acts 4:24). This church recognized the supreme importance of prayer.

The leaders prayed, the people prayed, and the church meeting was turned into a prayer meeting.

We must recognize the supreme importance of prayer. All of us must have a continuous desire to pray. We need to be like J. Hudson Taylor who stated: "The sun has never risen upon China without finding me at prayer. In forty years I saw 700 missionaries and 1,000 native workers in China."

II. In a Praying Church the Eyes of Faith and Expectancy Are Toward God

When the Jerusalem church had problems, they turned their eyes away from humankind and from the problems on hand; they looked to the Lord who can solve any problem and who is always in control of every situation. Luke recorded that these Christians "lifted up their voice to God with one accord, and said, Lord, thou art God, which hast made heaven, and earth, and the sea, and all that in them is" (Acts 4:24).

This was the approach of the psalmist as he wrote, "My soul, wait thou only upon God; for my expectation is from him" (62:5). Whatever problems face us, whatever problems we encounter, the only thing that ultimately matters is our fellowship with God, our being in touch with Him, finding His will, and being available to Him to come in with power and to work in and through us.

Sometimes the outlook may be bad, but it is the uplook that counts. In a certain cotton factory, there are cards on the walls of the workplace that read, "If your threads get tangled, send for the foreman." One day a new worker got her threads tangled; she tried to untangle them but only made them worse. Then she sent for the foreman.

He came and looked, then he asked her, "You've been doing this yourself?"

"Yes," she said.

"But, why did you not send for me according to instructions?"

"I did my best," she said.

"No, you did not," the foreman said. "Remember that doing your best is sending for me."

The eyes of a praying church are on God. He is the sovereign, self-revealing, and seeing Lord.

A. The Sovereign Lord

"Lord, thou art God, which hast made heaven, and earth, and the sea, and all that in them is: . . . For to do whatsoever thy hand and thy counsel determined before to be done" (4:24,28). In the beginning there was only God. He created the heavens and the earth. The universe is sustained in Him. Whatever God determines to be done will be done. He knows tomorrow's headlines and what will happen a day, a year, a century, and a millennium from now. He is the sovereign God. Jesus said, "All power is given unto me in heaven and in earth" (Matt. 28:18).

B. The Self-revealing Lord

We are told that when the disciples prayed, they quoted from the Old Testament Scriptures, and they reminded themselves of all that God had promised to do and all that He had already done. In verses 26 and 27, they recognized their dependence on God to reveal Himself to them. God had revealed Himself to them through the prophets and the kings such as David. Do you know God? Has God revealed Himself to you? He will as you read His Word, open your heart to His Spirit, and pray. Jesus said if anyone wills to do His will, "He shall know of the doctrine" (John 7:17).

C. The Seeing Lord

As these Christians prayed they said, "Lord, behold their threatenings" (Acts 4:29). These Jerusalem Christians were not looking at their problems, but they were looking at the power of Almighty God. They were not thinking about the possibility that Peter and John might be returned to prison; they lifted up their voice to God. They waited on Him. They expected God to do something.

When difficulties arise in our churches, what a difference it would make if we would get down on our knees together and wait before the Lord as these early Christians did.

A group of Christians in a rural area decided they would pray for much-needed rain. As they were going to the prayer meeting, a little girl brought a large umbrella. They wanted to know why she brought it: there wasn't a cloud in the sky. She was surprised; she said, "We are going to ask the Lord for rain, so I will need this umbrella on the way home." They were indulgent. When the prayer meeting was over, to their amazement and embarrassment, they heard the sound of thunder, and a heavy storm burst upon the area. The downpour continued all night. The little girl got home with dry clothes because of her firm belief in God's power that had not been clouded by skepticism. Our Lord said, "According to your faith be it unto you" (Matt. 9:29). This is still the divine decree.

III. In a Praying Church There Is a Desire to Evangelize

Verse 29 is the most challenging verse in this Scripture. "Now, Lord, . . . grant unto thy servants, that with all boldness they may speak thy word." As these disciples praised God who had brought the release of Peter and John, the burden of their prayer did not become a plea that He would now keep them safe. They pleaded to the Lord that He would enable them to go on proclaiming the gospel with greater courage. They didn't pray, "Lord, don't let it happen again." They prayed, "Lord, . . . grant unto thy servants that with all boldness they may speak thy word." In a praying church, we want to make salvation known to sinners.

It is relatively easy for some of us to stand before a group and tell them that Jesus saves. It seems to be more difficult to speak to one person and witness to that person about Christ. Yet many souls are won to Christ, one-on-one, as we speak to our family, our neighbors, and our friends about Jesus.

An associate of Billy Graham writes, "I'm an evangelist, and I have been witnessing and sharing my faith since I was fourteen years old. I've preached to crowds of 60,000 people, and, yet, I still get nervous when talking to an individual about Christ."

In a praying church there will be burdened hearts, burdened soul-winners, burdened sowers, and burdened reapers. Members will have a passion for souls and an earnest longing to make Christ known. The psalmist recorded the promise, "He that goeth forth and weepeth, bearing precious seed, shall doubtless come again with rejoicing, bringing his sheaves with him" (126:6).

The great preacher Henry Ward Beecher said, "The longer I live, the more confidence I have in those sermons preached where one man is the congregation." Mr. Beecher was talking about witnessing to the unsaved, seeking to win the lost to the Savior.

IV. In a Praying Church the Holy Spirit Manifests His Presence and Power

When the church prayed, the Holy Spirit manifested His presence and power. Acts records, "The place was shaken where they were assembled together; and they were all filled with the Holy Ghost, and they spake the word of God with boldness" (4:31). Prayer is the secret of every Pentecostal outpouring. We are not now considering what happened on the Day of Pentecost. The account in Acts chapter 4 is something that happened on another occasion after Pentecost. We are not told that the disciples were meeting together to pray specifically that they might be filled with the Holy Spirit. What they did was to get on their knees and ask the Lord to help them to be obedient to His commission and to be pleasing to Him as they sought to make the Lord Jesus known in the quickest possible way and to the largest possible number of people with the greatest possible results. As they prayed, the place was shaken, and they were all filled with the Holy Spirit. This can happen again and again.

There may never be another Day of Pentecost. But, there can and must be Pentecostal power and Pentecostal experiences in our lives and in the life of every church. We need the outpouring of the Holy Spirit. Why are we so slow to realize the importance of prayer and prayer meetings and praying as a church?

The Holy Spirit will move in miraculous ways in our midst. If you and I begin to pray individually and as the body of Christ, we will see miracles in the spiritual realm. We will see physical miracles. We will see people being saved. In Genesis 18:14 the question is asked:

"Is any thing too hard for the Lord?" When the church prays, God steps in and does great and mighty things (Acts 4:30).

V. In a Praying Church There Is Grace in the Lives of God's People

Luke told us that "great grace was upon them all" (Acts 4:33). The word *grace* here could be exchanged for the word *Christlikeness*. These people had the Spirit of Jesus Christ because they imitated the prayer life of the Savior.

First, God gave them the grace of unity. The Bible tells us that they had one heart and one soul (Acts 4:32). Because they prayed, they experienced the unity of the Spirit and the bond of peace (Eph. 4:3). They knew from experience the meaning of the words "ye are all one in Christ Jesus" (Gal. 3:28).

Second, there was the grace of renunciation. The church members were unselfish. They were willing to share their possessions. "Neither said any of them that ought of the things which he possessed was his own; but they had all things common" (Acts 4:32). What a marvelous inflowing and outflowing there was of the love of Christ! How greatly this is needed today! How is it achieved? It comes about as a direct result of the people of God learning to kneel down and pray together.

Third, there was the grace of liberality. There is a great need for Christians to be generous in their giving through the church. The Jerusalem church "had all things common" (Acts 4:32). In fact, Dr. Luke went on to report: "Neither was there any among them that lacked: for as many as were possessors of land or houses sold them, and brought the prices of the things that were sold, and laid them down at the apostles' feet: and distribution was made unto every man according as he had need" (Acts 4:34-35). In most churches 20 percent of the members give 80 percent of the money. How we need this grace of liberality.

In his excellent book *And Peter,* J. Wilbur Chapman tells the following story:

> A number of travelers were making their way across the desert. The last drop of water had been exhausted and they were pushing on with

the hope that more might be found. They were growing weaker and weaker. As a last resort they divided their men into companies and sent them on, one in advance of the other, in this way securing a rest they so much needed. If they who were in the advance guard were able to find the springs, they were to shout the good tidings to the men who were the nearest to them, and so they were to send the message along.

The long line reached far across the desert. They were fainting by the way when suddenly everyone was cheered by the good news. The leader of the first company had found the springs of water. He stood at the head of his men, shouting until the farthest man had heard his cry: "Water! Water!" The word went from man to man, until the whole company heard the sound, quickened their pace, and soon were drinking to their hearts' content![1]

We live in a dry and desolate place, a world where souls are desperately in need of the Water of life. Since we as believers have found that water in Christ, we have an obligation to share it with those who are dying of spiritual thirst. The cry should be ringing out from our lips, "Water! Water!" This invitation should be sounded everywhere: "Ho, every one that thirsteth, come ye to the waters" (Isa. 55:1). To do so is more than a solemn responsibility—it is an absolute necessity.

1. J. Wilbur Chapman, *And Peter* (New York: Fleming H. Revell Co., 1895), 84.

8
The Church Needs Leaders

(Acts 6:1-8)

The life of a local church cannot rise above the level of its leaders. Someone has written: "Like pastor, like people; like teachers, like students; like deacon, like member." It becomes essential, therefore, that those upon whom God has placed the responsibility of leadership should be well qualified. Church leaders should not only possess eternal life, but life more abundant.

Satan hurls many obstacles in the path of a growing church. The treasurer of the first church betrayed the Lord, stole the offerings, and then committed suicide. The church continued to grow. The apostles were imprisoned, beaten, and threatened, but the church continued to grow. Two prominent members of the church, Ananias and Sapphira, were hypocrites. They lied about their offerings, but the church continued to grow. Then there arose dissension inside the church as they argued over the benevolence fund, and church growth stopped. The church can overcome the devil's opposition from without, but it can never afford division within the fellowship.

When the disciples saw that the church fellowship was threatened, they called the congregation together and proposed a solution. The congregation would select seven spiritually qualified leaders. These leaders would handle the ministry of benevolence. The apostles then would give themselves to praying and proclaiming the Word of God.

The church family liked this solution. They selected seven men who were honest, Spirit filled, and wise. They laid their hands on them and prayed for the ministry they would perform.

Many believe that these men were the first deacons ordained by the church. We know for certain that they were the first church leaders selected by the congregation in the New Testament. The result of their ministry was miraculous. A great number of people were saved, miracles took place, and it was evident that God was blessing the church because some of the priests were also converted (Acts 6:7-8).

The church needs leaders today! What are the qualities that should characterize those who hold office in the church? In Acts 6 the church leaders are described as being saved, select, sincere, steadfast, and spiritual.

I. Saved

No one is qualified to hold an elective office in the church until that individual has received Jesus Christ as his or her personal Savior. This basic requirement for church leadership is stated in Acts 6:3: "Wherefore, brethren, look ye out among you."

The Bible teaches that these first-ordained leaders were to be selected from the membership of the church. In the early church, the members of the church were regenerate, born again. The Bible tells us in Acts 2 that they had repented of their sins (v. 38). Peter preached on the Day of Pentecost that people needed to repent of their sin and trust Christ as Savior. Those who were in the Jerusalem church gladly received the word of Simon Peter that Jesus was the Savior and that they needed to turn to Him in faith in order to be saved. Luke went on to tell us that those who received the preaching of Peter that Jesus had been resurrected and was the Savior were added to the church (Acts 2:47).

One of the tragic weaknesses of many churches is that good men and women have been placed in office, but they have never been born again. When it comes to choosing leaders for any position of responsibility in the church, the first questions we should ask are: Has this person a clear testimony to the saving grace of God? and Does this person's life give evidence of a true change of heart?

The great author Walter B. Knight delights to tell the story of Timmy, his cat. The family loved Timmy. There was one thing, however, that they disliked in Timmy—he preyed on the birds that nested in the trees in the backyard.

One day Timmy was eating a robin. Knight snatched the unconsumed portion of the bird from the cat. He sprinkled it with red pepper. Then he dangled the morsel temptingly before the cat. Instantly the cat's sharp teeth closed on it, only to drop it the next instant! The cat sputtered and ran away, meowing.

Did that rather drastic procedure break the cat's habit of catching and killing more birds? No. It was the cat's nature to catch birds. Knight could not break Timmy's bad habit by working on him *externally*.

The heart is deceitful and desperately wicked. It is human nature to sin. For confirmation read your daily newspaper. Lopping off a twig or a branch here and there does not change humanity's sinful nature. We must be changed *inwardly* before we will act right *outwardly*. Not external reformation, but inward regeneration is the answer to the human sin question. George Whitefield, when asked why he preached so often on the text, "Ye must be born again," replied that it was because ye must be born again.

II. Select

The kind of leaders that the church needs must be very carefully selected. The disciples instructed the early church to "look ye out" (Acts 6:3). Here we learn that the democratic ideal was practiced in the apostolic church. The apostles said to the members, "You look out for men whom we may appoint." The whole church was invited to participate in the selection of suitable men to serve as the first leaders. This was not the decision of Peter alone, nor even of the apostles only, but rather all of the members were privileged to share in this letter.

This passage leads us to pause and remind ourselves how serious and how solemn a business it is to exercise any influence over or to cast a vote in favor of the appointment of anyone into any position of responsibility in the Lord's work. The seriousness of the church's business arises from the fact that it can be made or marred, advanced, or retarded by the quality of men and women who are placed into office.

We learn from this passage that people should be selected only after much prayer. In Acts 6:6 Luke reported, "Whom they set before the apostles: and when they had prayed, they laid their hands on them."

The church today desperately needs people who will work for the Lord Jesus Christ. Someone has said that in the church there are two kinds of members: workers and shirkers. There are those who are willing to do anything, and there are those who are willing for the others to do everything. There are three kinds of people: those who make things happen, those who watch things happen, and those who have no idea of what has happened.

It is the moral and spiritual responsibility of every member of the church to have a definite place where that individual seeks to serve the Lord Jesus Christ. On the other hand, it is the responsibility of the congregation as a whole to prayerfully consider who will be elected to hold specific offices in the church.

Phillips Brooks was a great preacher. One day he said:

> Oh, do not pray for easy lives. Pray to be strong men and women. Do not pray for tasks equal to your powers. Pray for powers equal to your tasks. Then the doing of your work will be no miracle; but you shall be a miracle. Every day you shall wonder at yourself, at the richness of life which has come to you by the grace of God.

Would you say: "I am but one, but I am one. I cannot do everything, but I can do something. What I can do, I ought to do. And what I ought to do, with God's help, I will do."

III. Sincere

The early church sought men of good reputation to be their leaders. The Bible tells us that they were to be "seven men of honest report" (Acts 6:3). They had to have a good reputation in the church and in the world as well. It is quite possible to have a good reputation in the church and a bad reputation in the office, shop, or in one's neighborhood.

Some people are on their best behavior when they're in the house of God. They seem to be far less particular when they are engaged in the daily routine of everyday life. Men and women who are leaders in the church are to be utterly sincere, thoroughly honest in all of their words and in their dealings with others.

Great damage can be done to the church when men and women of bad or indifferent reputation are given leadership positions in the church. In selecting leaders for the church, these questions should be asked:

Is the person respected by friends and coworkers?

Is the individual consistent in Christian living?

Is he or she God-fearing and reliable?

Is he or she a person of spiritual and moral integrity?

Christianity is more often caught than taught. The great Pentecostal evangelist, Bud Robinson, was right when he said: "I don't care how loud a brother shouts or how high he jumps, just so he walks straight when he comes down." Amen!

There are a number of admonitions in the Bible telling us how we ought to walk in sincerity:

"Walk in newness of life" (Rom. 6:4).

"Walk honestly" (Rom. 13:13).

"Walk in the Spirit" (Gal. 5:16).

"Walk worthy of the vocation" (Eph. 4:1).

"Walk in love" (Eph. 5:2).

"Walk as children of light" (Eph. 5:8).

"Walk circumspectly" (Eph. 5:15).

"Walk worthy of the Lord" (Col. 1:10).

"Walk in wisdom" (Col. 4:5).

"Walk worthy of God" (1 Thess. 2:12).

"Walk . . . to please God" (1 Thess. 4:1).

"Walk even as he walked" (1 John 2:6).

A person's Sunday self and his or her weekday self are like two halves of a round-trip ticket: not good if detached. If Christ is the center of our lives, the circumference will take care of itself. Christianity is either relevant all of the time or useless any time. It is not just a phase of life, it is life itself.

On one occasion, Fritz Kriesler had several hours to spend between trains in a certain city. He decided to walk around to see the sights. He stopped in front of a music store and saw in the window something he wanted to purchase. He went into the store and laid his violin case with his name on it on the counter. The shopkeeper saw the name on the case and thought that the famous musician's violin had been stolen by the man. He excused himself and, going back to the office, called the police. Soon they came and accused this man of stealing Kriesler's violin. He insisted that he was Kriesler, but they would not believe him. Finally, he said to the shopkeeper, "Do you have one of Fritz Kriesler's recordings in your shop?" "Yes," replied the man.

"Please play the number for me," said Kriesler, "and then I will play the same number on my violin." They listened to the music that had been recorded by Kriesler. Then he picked up the violin and played the piece. The shopkeeper and the policeman stood in amazement. They knew then that he was Kriesler, so they apologized to him profusely and let him go. You see, his performance measured up to his profession! Church leaders need to be sincere— without wax or gloss.

IV. Steadfast

The church needs leaders that are steadfast. When the early church selected their leaders, the Bible says, "They chose Stephen, a man full of faith." This is God's way of saying that Stephen was very steadfast in his commitment to Jesus Christ. That must be the sterling characteristic of the church leader. He or she must be a man or a woman of faith. Jesus told us to be faithful unto death, and He will give to us a crown of life.

Stephen witnessed so faithfully before the Sanhedrin that they could not bear to hear his testimony. They held their hands over their ears. They led him just beyond the walls of the city. Wicked men with cruel hands picked up hard stones and killed Stephen. In his dying moments, he breathed a prayer, calling upon God and saying, "Lord Jesus, receive my spirit" (Acts 7:59). He then knelt down and, following the perfect example of Jesus, prayed that God would forgive the very men that stoned him, saying, "Lord, lay not this sin to their charge." Then he died.

The prayer of every sincere Christian worker should be: "Lord, help me to be steadfast. Help me not to be weary in well doing." Those who are faithful in well doing need not fear those who are spiteful and evildoing, for they have a God to trust who has well doers under the control of His protection and even evildoers under the hand of His restraint.

V. Spiritual

Above all, the church needs leaders who are spiritual. When the apostles were admonishing the church regarding the kind of men that they ought to select, they said "Look ye out among you seven men of honest report, full of the Holy Ghost and wisdom, whom we may appoint over this business" (Acts 6:3). The supreme qualification of those who were chosen is that they were Spirit-filled. This is a high standard. It is God's standard. In all the work of our churches let us not lower God's standard. The first qualification required for any man or woman who is to be a worker in the Lord's vineyard is not popularity, seniority, or even ability, but spirituality!

How can we tell when people are spiritual? Is there a way that we can know whether or not a man or a woman is filled with the Holy Spirit? There most assuredly is. The Bible tells us, "The fruit of the Spirit is love, joy, peace, longsuffering, gentleness, goodness, faith, meekness, temperance: against such there is no law" (Gal. 5:22-23).

When a person is filled with the Holy Spirit, that individual is right within himself. He or she has love, joy, and peace. That individual is also in a right relationship with other people because the fruit of the Spirit is longsuffering, gentleness, and goodness. But more than that, the individual is rightly related to God, for the fruit of the Spirit is "faith, meekness, and temperance."

Organization in the church without the Holy Spirit is like a mill without power. Even a church that is thoroughly orthodox and accepts biblical standards is as useless as are clouds without rain, until endued with Power from on high.

Resolve to be a worker for Christ serving Him through His

church. The New Testament standard in Acts 6 is that you be saved, select, sincere, steadfast, and spiritual. This is the kind of leader God can and will use.

9
The Christian God Uses

(Acts 9:10-17)

One of the most humbling truths revealed in the Word of God is that God uses you and me for the accomplishment of His purposes. That is a staggering thought. The infinite, eternal, omniscient, omnipresent God uses folks like you and me to do His work on earth.

One man who was wonderfully used by the Lord was Ananias. He was privileged to seek out and lead Saul of Tarsus into an understanding of what God wanted the great apostle to do. We read about Ananias only twice in the New Testament, in chapters 9 and 22 of Acts. He is presented to us as the type of Christian God can use.

I. A Member of the Body of Christ

The Christian God uses must be a member of the body of Christ. God works through Christians who, by the miracle of the new birth and baptism of the Holy Spirit, have been made members of the body of Christ. Jesus told Nicodemus that one needs the new birth to be a member of God's kingdom (John 3:3). When a person is converted, a number of things happen. One is that the Holy Spirit baptizes us into the body of Christ. "For by one Spirit are we all baptized into one body" (1 Cor. 12:13).

The clear teaching of the New Testament is that of a general church and a local church. A person becomes a member of the *general church* by trusting Christ as Savior. The moment a Christian is saved, he or she is baptized by the Holy Spirit into the body of Christ. The baptism of the Holy Spirit occurs at conversion, can never be repeated, and is positional, not experiential.

An individual becomes a member of a *local* congregation by trusting Christ as Savior and publicly confessing Christ by believer's baptism. Acts 2:41 gives the divine order: "Then they that gladly received his Word were baptized: and the same day there were added unto them about three thousand souls."

Jesus clearly told Saul of Tarsus that in persecuting Christians he had been persecuting the Lord Himself, for believers are members of the body of Christ (Acts 9:4-5). Jesus is the Head of the church, and we, as members of the church, are members of Christ's body. Thus, the disciples of the Lord and the Lord Himself are one.

During His earthly ministry, our Lord had an earthly body. He lived and worked through that earthly body. Now Jesus is in heaven, and Jesus' body on earth is the church. From heaven, Jesus the Head, works through individual members of His body, the church (1 Cor. 12:12-13).

Ananias, a member of that body, was greatly used by the Lord. If you and I are to be used by the Lord, the same must be true of us. Have you been converted? Have you followed Christ in New Testament believer's baptism? Are you a member of a local church where you are actively working for Christ?

Once a man asked the question, "Can I be a Christian without joining the church?" I thought about that a long time. The answer is yes, you can be a Christian without joining the church, but that would be like being:

- a student who will not go to school,
- a soldier who will not join the army,
- a citizen who does not pay taxes or vote,
- a salesman with no customers,
- an explorer with no base camp,
- a seaman on a ship without a crew,
- a businessman on a deserted island,
- an author without readers,
- a tuba player without an orchestra,
- a parent without a family,
- a football player without a team,
- a politician who is a hermit,
- a scientist who does not share his findings, and
- a bee without a hive.

Yes, you can be a Christian without being a member of the church, but it's completely abnormal, and you'll never be a Spirit-filled Christian used of God until you become a member of a local church.

II. Probably a Very Unlikely Person

The Christian God uses will probably be a very unlikely person. God used Ananias to do a tremendous thing. Ananias led Saul of Tarsus to understand how to become a Christian, helped him to receive the filling of the Holy Spirit, led him to be baptized, and encouraged him to associate with the local church. The whole ministry of the apostle Paul was launched by a disciple named Ananias about whom we know very little. He is simply called "a certain disciple" (Acts 9:10). He was not an apostle, was probably not an outstanding man, and as far as we know was not even a deacon or a teacher. He is simply "a certain disciple." God delights to use ordinary people, and this is a great encouragement to all of us (1 Cor. 1:26-29).

It was Nathan, a little-known prophet, who led David to repentance. It was a little maid who reached Naaman, the captain of the Syrian host. When God wanted to lead Saul of Tarsus into the assurance of salvation, he used "a certain disciple" named Ananias. God can use you!

When I was a young boy attending the Second Baptist Church in Hot Springs, Arkansas, a godly man taught our nine-year-old boys' Sunday School class. Since they couldn't get another teacher, he taught our class from the time I was nine until I was twelve. He did not speak very well and could hardly read, but he loved the Lord Jesus. He shared that love with those of us in the class. What was the result of his teaching? One of the members in the class became an attorney and a judge. Another class member became a wonderful postal employee. A couple of the members of the class became outstanding businessmen. Three of the members of the class became preachers of the gospel. All of the members of the class are still active in the church today. Not a single member of that boys' class was ever arrested.

If God can use my Sunday School teacher to transform a class of boys and if God can use a certain disciple named Ananias to lead Paul, the apostle, into the deeper walk of the Christian life, don't you know that God can use you? Most of the time, the Christian God uses is a very ordinary person.

III. Living a Devout Christian Life

The Christian God uses must be living a devout Christian life. The Bible speaks of Ananias being "a devout man" (Acts 22:12). It goes on to state that he had "a good report of all the Jews." This simply means that Ananias was a devout Christian. There was no insincerity about his life or testimony. He "adorned the doctrines of Christ"; that is he incarnated the teachings of the Bible in flesh and blood.

There was a sixteen-year-old girl who was a chronic invalid. Her mother was a pleasure-loving woman who could not endure the idea of being with her shut-in daughter. While the mother was traveling abroad in Italy, she remembered the coming birthday of her daughter and sent her a rare and beautiful vase. The trained nurse brought it to the girl saying that her mother had sent it so carefully that it came right on her birthday. After looking at its beauty for a moment, the girl turned to the nurse and said, "Take it away, take it away! Oh, mother, do not send me anything more—no books, no flowers, no pictures, no vases. I want you!"

That must be the pleading cry of the Savior. Don't give Christ things—He wants *you*. Jesus wants your yielded heart, your heart fully given. He knows that all else will follow.

IV. Utterly at God's Disposal

The Christian God uses must be utterly at God's disposal. Ananias was living in such close touch with the Lord that he could hear Jesus speaking. The Lord said, "Ananias," and he said, "Behold, I am here, Lord" (Acts 9:10).

Ananias was on speaking terms with the Lord. Are you? Acts 9:10-16 reveals the intimate conversation that went on between Ananias and Jesus. The Lord asked Ananias to go (v. 15) and Ananias went (v. 17). There was complete obedience.

A man recorded his meeting with General William Booth, founder of the Salvation Army, with these words:

> When I looked into his face and saw him brush back his hair from his brow, heard him speak of the trials and the conflicts and the victories, I said "General Booth, tell me what has been the secret of your success." He hesitated a second, and I saw the tears come into his eyes and steal down his cheeks, and then he said, "I'll tell you the secret. God has had all there was of me to have. There have been men with greater opportunities; but from the day I got the poor of London on my heart and a vision of what Jesus Christ could do, I made up my mind that God would have all there was of William Booth, and if there's anything of power in the Salvation Army today, it is because God has had all the adoration of my heart, all the power of my will, and all the influence of my life."

The listener reported: "I learned from William Booth that the greatness of a man's power was in the measure of his surrender."[1]

V. Full of Christlike Love

The Christian God uses must be full of Christlike love. When Ananias went to Saul he did not say, "You scoundrel, you persecutor of the church! You've done much evil!"

What did Ananias say? And what was his attitude? He put his arm around Saul and said, "Brother Saul" (v. 17). There was great love and compassion in those words.

This is a test of our Christianity. When you are harmed and hurt by another Christian, are you able to go and say "Brother"?

Brian Green tells that at the last meeting of one of his evangelistic campaigns in America, he asked the people to stand up and in a few words say what the revival had done for them. A black girl rose. She was not a good speaker. She could only put a few sentences together, and this is what she said: "Through this campaign I have found Christ, and He made me able to forgive the man who murdered my father."

"He made me able to forgive"—that is the very essence of Christianity. Through Christ, Saul and Ananias—men who had been the bitterest enemies—came together as brothers.

Jesus taught us to pray, "Forgive us our trespasses, as we forgive those who trespass against us." The Bible admonishes us to be kind, tenderhearted, forgiving one another even as God for Christ's sake has forgiven us. We need Christ's love in our hearts.

VI. Lead Others to Blessing

The Christian God uses should lead others into the blessings of Christianity. On the threshold of his new life, Ananias led Saul into the fullness of spiritual blessing, for he showed him how to be filled with the Holy Spirit (Acts 9:17).

Ananias knew how imperative it is for any Christian to be filled with the Holy Spirit if he or she is to live graciously and serve God effectively. At Pentecost Christians were filled with the Holy Spirit (Acts 2:4). The filling of the Holy Spirit is as essential to the Christian life as gasoline is to an automobile. God commands us to be filled with the Holy Spirit (Eph. 5:18).

Mendelssohn once visited a cathedral containing one of the most priceless organs in Europe. He listened to the organist and then asked permission to play. "I don't know you," was the reply. "And we don't allow any chance stranger to play upon this organ."

At last, the great musician persuaded the organist to let him play. As Mendelssohn played, the great cathedral was filled with such music as the organist had never heard. With tears in his eyes, he laid his hand on Mendelssohn's shoulder. "Who are you?" he asked. "Mendelssohn," came the reply.

The old organist was dumbfounded. "To think," he said, "the master was here, and I nearly forbade him to play upon my organ!"

If we only knew what wonderful, harmonious service the Holy Spirit can draw out of our lives, we would not be content until He has complete possession and is working in us and through us to do His will.

1. Walter B. Knight, *Three Thousand Illustrations for Christian Service* (Grand Rapids, Mich.: Wm. B. Eerdmans, 1957), 169.

10
When You Come to Church

(Isa. 6:1-8)

At the end of Woody Allen's film on human relationships, *Annie Hall*, Woody tells the old story about the man who thought he was a chicken. His wife went to a psychiatrist for some help in dealing with her husband's problem. After she had explained her husband's behavior to the doctor, he said, "That's ridiculous! Why don't you tell him he's not a chicken?" The woman immediately responded, "Because I need the eggs!"

Sometimes Christians are asked about the headaches of maintaining a strong and enduring church membership. They are asked, "Why go to the bother of attending church?" The answer is, "We need the eggs!" Most of us have needs that can only be met in a church relationship. Not only friendship needs or service needs are met, but so also are needs of worship, cleansing, security, and assurance. That was certainly Isaiah's experience.

King Uzziah died, and young Isaiah's heart was broken. The king had been a friend to the young student. The stability of the nation depended on the king. The nation was in mourning. It seemed as if Isaiah's world had stopped.

Perhaps you have had a similar experience. A loved one has died, or you are concerned about the condition of the nation. We reach those times in our lives when our spirits are crushed within us. We can associate with Isaiah's grief and sorrow.

What did Isaiah do when he faced a crisis? He went immediately to the house of God! That is what you and I should do as we face the difficulties of life. We should go to church. What should we experience when we come to church?

I. When You Come to Church You Should Behold Your God

Isaiah greatly admired King Uzziah. He loved and reverenced the king. Uzziah was a great king. He had ruled the land of Judah for fifty-two years. He organized the army, fortified Jerusalem, and defeated the Philistines and Arabians. Uzziah promoted agriculture and building projects. He had a deep faith in Jehovah.

But Uzziah was human. He made the mistake of leaving the pagan places of worship standing. Later, Uzziah's pride became his downfall. He went into the temple to offer an incense sacrifice to God. This was a work that only the priest could perform. When Uzziah sinned in this manner, he was immediately stricken with leprosy. He never recovered. When the king died, the news was heralded throughout the kingdom, "The king is dead!"

Isaiah was shaken. His king was gone. He lifted his eyes beyond the mortal remains of his earthly king to the heavenly King. He saw God! Isaiah did not have this vision of God until King Uzziah died. But when Uzziah died, Isaiah saw God!

Sometimes we are guilty of putting other people or things in the place of God. Often these people or things must become secondary before we can see God in all of His resplendent glory and power. Some never see God until death knocks at the door of the home. Many never call on God until their riches are stripped away or health is broken. Broken and battered, we find ourselves looking beyond ourselves and this earth to the Heavenly Father.

Isaiah told of his experience: "I saw also the Lord sitting upon a throne, high and lifted up, and his train filled the temple" (Isa. 6:1). What a revelation Isaiah had of God's glory! First, he beheld Jesus in His preincarnate glory. Isaiah saw the glory that Jesus possessed before He came to be our suffering Savior when divinity was wrapped in swaddling clothes.

The earthly throne of Judah was empty for King Uzziah had died, but Isaiah saw Jesus reigning, "sitting upon a throne" (v. 1). How wonderful it is in days of uncertainty to know that there is a throne established in heaven forever and that Jesus reigns upon that throne. "Thy throne, O God, is for ever and ever" (Ps. 45:6).

Looking into heaven, Isaiah saw that Jesus Christ was being worshiped. He wrote, "I saw also the Lord . . . high and lifted up" (v. 1). He saw the seraphims with their six wings. These magnificent angelic creatures were utterly humbled in Christ's presence, covering their faces and feet. They were prepared to immediately carry out the Lord's commands symbolized by the wings that enabled them to fly swiftly. They cried, "Holy, holy, holy, is the Lord of hosts: the whole earth is full of his glory" (6:3).

When these angelic beings worshiped Jesus, they covered their faces because the purity of our Lord was so dazzling. They recognized His power, saying, "The whole earth is full of his glory." They referred to Him as "the Lord of hosts," meaning that He commanded all of the angels of heaven.

When Isaiah saw this majestic scene, he exclaimed: "Mine eyes have seen the King" (6:5). Moreover, he recognized that one day the kingdoms of this earth would be the kingdoms of our Lord and Savior Jesus Christ and that He would reign forever and ever. Isaiah saw Jesus' future glory and the seraphim exclaiming: "The whole earth is full of his glory" (6:3).

When Isaiah had a vision of God, he caught a glimpse of the Trinity. The angelic host said, "Holy, holy, holy, is the Lord of hosts." This is a reference to God as Holy Father, Holy Son, and Holy Spirit. Christians believe that there is one God and that He is Father, Son, and Spirit. When God created human beings, He said, "Let *us* make man in our image" (emphasis mine). And when God spoke to Isaiah, He said, "Whom shall I send, and who will go for *us?*" (emphasis mine). These are obvious references to the Trinity.

When we behold God, we begin to understand that holiness is a central attribute of the Almighty. Holiness is Deity. It is synonymous with the name of God. The seraphims are described as having six wings. With two they covered their face, symbolizing humility in the presence of God's holiness. With two wings they covered their feet, symbolizing defilement in the presence of God's holiness. And with two wings they did fly, symbolizing obedience and willingness to do that which the holy God commands. Isaiah said he saw the Lord high and lifted up. He was describing Jesus lifted up in His power, love, knowledge, omniscience, omnipotence, and omnipresence.

A small lad one day came to his father and said, "Dad, have you seen God?" The father replied: "Son, no one has ever seen God. God is invisible to the human eye." The little boy left the room disheartened.

The pastor of the church came into the home to visit. While he was there, the lad asked him, "Pastor, have you ever seen God?" The kind minister responded: "Son, God is a spirit. A spirit is invisible to the eye. No one can see God." The little boy again was disappointed.

Soon the father found the little lad spending a lot of his spare time with an old sailor down by the waterfront. Every day he visited the man late in the afternoon. The boy's father became concerned about him for he feared a sailor's influence on his son. The father said, "Son, I wish you wouldn't spend so much time with the old sailor." The boy replied: "Dad, he tells me to obey you and mother, go to church, and study hard in school. He teaches me good manners, and he tells me about the wonderful adventures he's had. He's a nice man, a good man, a kind man, but most of all he's a Christian. Please let me continue to visit with him."

The father was surprised, but with a smile he said, "Son, it's fine for you to visit with him as often as you like if he is teaching you those things."

One afternoon at sunset, the little boy and the sailor were sitting at the waterfront talking. After their conversation ended, there was a long silence, the kind that can come between two friends when there is a lull. The boy looked at the old sailor and asked, "Have you ever seen God?"

The sailor looked at the boy and then out across the water as the sun was nestling itself in its orbit like a child being nestled in the cradle at the end of the day. He saw the last fiery sparks being thrown out across the universe by the sun. The sunset was resplendent in glory. A seagull gently dipped into the sea below, emerging with a fish. The waves were washing up on the shore, and all the ocean was alive with the presence and the power of the Almighty. The boy thought the sailor didn't hear the question. He repeated it,

"Sir, have you ever seen God?" The old sailor looked at the lad and, as a tear welled up in his eye, he responded, "Son, it's getting to the place where I can hardly see anything else!"

When we come to church, we ought to behold our God!

II. When You Come to Church You Should Confess Your Sins

How important it is that we realize our shortcomings and sins. Once a person really beholds God, that individual will repent as did Isaiah. Listen to Isaiah's confession: "Woe is me! for I am undone" (6:5). This is an essential part of every worship service. We must remember that God is God and that we are weak, sinful, human flesh. Even at our best we are unprofitable servants in His presence.

A. We Should Confess Personal Shortcomings

When young Isaiah came to church and entered into the presence of God, he recognized his personal shortcomings. He cried, "Woe is me! for I am undone." He confessed himself to be a man of unclean lips. Speech is a true test of what we are. The word that a person speaks reveals what that person is. Jesus said, "Out of the abundance of the heart the mouth speaketh" (Matt. 12:34). What we say with our lips reveals what is in our hearts.

Few of us are wise enough or disciplined enough to control the words that we speak when the heart is wrong. The writer of the Book of James stated, "If any man offend not in word, the same is a perfect man, and able also to bridle the whole body" (3:2). James said that a test of our character is revealed by the words we speak.

Uncle Bud Robinson was a great gospel evangelist. A woman with a wicked tongue came down during the invitation to rededicate her life to Christ. She said to Uncle Bud, "I want to lay my tongue upon the altar." The evangelist knew her evil habit of gossiping, and he said, "Lady, go ahead, the altar is only sixteen-feet long, but lay all of your tongue you can upon it." Sins of the tongue need to be confessed!

B. We Should Confess the Sins of People Around Us

Worshiping God, Isaiah experienced dissatisfaction with people that lived around him. Previously, the things that they had done had been acceptable in his sight. But once Isaiah came into the presence of God and had a real worship experience, his concept of society was changed.

We are not to be busybodies, meddling in other people's affairs. We are, however, to be concerned about the world in which we live. We need to pray earnestly for the blessing of God on people who have wandered far outside the will of God. When we come to church, we need to confess the sins of the nation, the state, the city, and the neighborhood in which we live. We too dwell in the midst of a people of unclean lips.

III. When You Come to Church You Should Receive God's Forgiveness

Seeing God and confessing his sins, Isaiah experienced the forgiveness of the Almighty. A seraphim took a live coal from the altar and said, "Lo, this hath touched thy lips; and thine iniquity is taken away, and thy sin purged" (6:7).

The seraphim represents the Holy Spirit. The live coal represents the blood of Christ. The altar represents the cross. The Holy Spirit takes the blood of Christ from the altar of God and applies it to our hearts. This cleanses us of sin.

In the Old Testament, the altar was a place of sacrifice. It symbolized the forgiveness of sin. You and I need to come to the altar of God and ask that our sins be forgiven. The three hardest words in the English language to pronounce are, "I have sinned!"

Not far from New York is a cemetery where there is a grave with just one word inscribed on its headstone: "Forgiven." There is no name, no date of birth or death. The stone is not embellished by the sculptor's art. There is no epithet, no fulsome eulogy, just that one word, "Forgiven." But, that is the greatest thing that can be written on the gravestone of any man or woman, "Forgiven."

IV. When You Come to Church You Should Volunteer for Service

What a tremendous experience Isaiah had as he went to the temple. He beheld God! He confessed his sins! He experienced cleansing forgiveness! The natural result of all of this is that he was used by God. He became the greatest writing prophet of the Old Testament.

When Isaiah heard the voice of God saying, "Whom shall I send, and who will go for us?" he responded, "Here am I; send me" (6:8). The closing part of any worship experience should always lead to dedication on our part to the service of Jesus Christ. Worship is not something that is held for convenience or as a matter of habit. Worship should change our hearts and minds and make us servants of others and, most importantly, servants of God.

One day a lady approaching the worship service found that she was late. Just as she stepped up to the doors, they were opened by the ushers, and the people started leaving the sanctuary. The woman asked, "Is the service over?" The usher responded with all due wisdom, "Worship is over—the service is just beginning."

When the hour of worship ends, our service to God should begin. As we go from church, we should be saying with Isaiah, "Here am I, Lord; send me."

11
The Mystery of Tithing

(Lev. 27:30-32; 2 Cor. 8:7-9)

One of the mysterious subjects in the Bible is tithing. It is like prayer in many ways. Praying is an act of worship, and so is tithing. Prayer is taught in the Scriptures and commanded of God, so is tithing. In order for a person to understand prayer, he or she must experience the joy of it. So is it true that in order for a person to understand tithing, he or she must experience it by giving God a minimum of one-tenth of his or her income. Tithing, indeed, is a very mysterious subject. It is such a glorious mystery that it is hidden from the eyes of many people.

First you must commit yourself totally to God. Determine that you are going to let God rule every part of your life. Jesus said that where our treasure is, there will our hearts be also. So, if you want your heart to be in the hands of God, you first have to commit your treasure. That is the mystery of tithing. It is a humble commitment of faith of oneself to God.

I. There Is a Mystery about the Origin of Tithing

When did tithing originate? Some believe tithing started when Moses gave the law to the Jews in the desert of Arabia. Closer study, however, reveals that Moses simply incorporated the tithe into the law. The people of God were tithing long before the day of Moses. Tithing had been a practice for years when Moses, by the divine command of God, placed the law of tithes and offerings in the Levitical commandments.

Abraham lived at least five hundred years before Moses. The Bible tells us that he was a tither. The first recorded act of tithing in the

Bible is found in Genesis 14:20: "Blessed be the most high God, which hath delivered thine enemies into thy hand. And he gave him tithes of all." Abraham had won a military victory. He had rescued his nephew Lot. The mysterious priest, Melchizedek, appeared on the scene. In order to show his gratitude to God, Abraham gave a tithe of everything he had captured in the battle. Tithing must have been a time-honored and ancient custom, even in the day of Abraham.

It is possible that God instructed Adam to tithe. It has been suggested that the offerings made by Cain and Abel to God were the result of God's divine command given to their father Adam. The first recorded act of worship on the part of both Cain and Abel is bringing their offerings to the Lord. Genesis 4:3 states: "In the process of time it came to pass, that Cain brought of the fruit of the ground an offering unto the Lord. And Abel, he also brought of the firstlings of his flock and of the fat thereof. And the Lord had respect unto Abel and to his offering."

Human beings were being shown at the beginning that they were accountable to God for their stewardship. Thus from the first, people have been commanded to invest a portion of their income in the work of the kingdom of God. God taught Adam and his children to bring an offering to the Lord.

Why would God teach people in the first book of the Bible to bring offerings to God? I believe God wanted to remind us that one day we are going to travel to a distant country, heaven. He wants us to make the correct transfer of our funds before we go. The only way to change the money of this earth into the treasures of heaven is to give to God while we are here on earth. It remains true: "What I have, I lost. What I gave away, I kept forever."

II. There Is a Mystery about the Persistency of Tithing

The plan of tithing revealed to us in the Bible originated with the Almighty. Were tithing not of God, it would have been discontinued long ago. But, since tithing is God's plan, it will continue throughout the centuries. It will continue to be the practice of the children of God until Jesus comes.

Recall the revelation of the progressive teaching of tithing found in the Bible. The first recorded act of tithing is found in Genesis 14:20 when it is said regarding Abraham, "He gave him tithes of all."

Jacob continued the practice of tithing. He stated, "This stone, which I have set for a pillar, shall be God's house: and of all that thou shalt give me I will surely give the tenth unto thee" (Gen. 28:22). Moses incorporated tithing into the law. He taught the people what God had commanded, "All the tithe of the land, whether of the seed of the land, or of the fruit of the tree, is the Lord's: it is holy unto the Lord" (Lev. 27:30). In that same passage of Scripture, Moses went on to say, "The tenth shall be holy unto the Lord" (v. 32).

The last writing prophet in the Old Testament was Malachi. With great fervor he preached to the people the message of God. In a straightforward manner he condemned the people for forsaking the practice of tithing. The prophet Malachi wrote:

> Will a man rob God? Yet ye have robbed me. But ye say, Wherein have we robbed thee? In tithes and offerings. Ye are cursed with a curse: for ye have robbed me, even this whole nation. Bring ye all the tithes into the storehouse, that there may be meat in mine house, and prove me now herewith, saith the Lord of Hosts, if I will not open you the windows of heaven, and pour you out a blessing, that there shall not be room enough to receive it (3:8-10).

As you study the progression of tithing in the Bible, you are struck with the fact that Jesus, our Savior, practiced tithing. He perfectly kept the law. Indeed, Jesus commended tithing while condemning omitting judgment, mercy, and faith. "Woe unto you, scribes and Pharisees, hypocrites! for ye pay tithe of mint and anise and cummin, and have omitted the weightier matters of the law, judgment, mercy, and faith: these ought ye to have done, and not to leave the other undone" (Matt. 23:23).

A very clear explanation of how we are to bring our tithes to God is outlined by the apostle Paul in 1 Corinthians 16:2, "Upon the first day of the week let every one of you lay by him in store, as God hath prospered him, that there be no gatherings when I come." Paul told us that each individual ("let every one of you") is to bring his or her tithe on Sunday ("the first day") to the church ("in store"). Our giving is to be a percentage of increase ("as God hath prospered"). This should alleviate the need for endless special offerings ("that there be no gatherings when I come"). There can be no clearer way of stating what we are to do in our giving and when we are to do it, as well as where we are to bring our offerings.

The Bible goes on to teach that Jesus now receives our tithes. When we give our tithes through the church, we are not giving to people but rather to Jesus, our Savior. Hebrews 7:8 states, "Here men that die receive tithes; but there he receiveth them, of whom it is witnessed that he liveth." The writer of Hebrews was telling how the priest received tithes in former days. Now the one who receives our tithes is no one less than Jesus Christ who lives forever in heaven with God.

The method of supporting our churches today is through the tithes and offerings of God's people. We should not depend on human schemes to secure money. Churches are ill advised to sponsor pie suppers, bingo, raffles, or an endless string of fund-raising events to do the work of God. We should tell the people of God of the great needs of the kingdom and trust the Lord to lay on the hearts of His people to dedicate their tithes and offerings to the work of God through the church.

A flour miller tried to get the members of his country church to tithe. Many of them made excuses that they could not live on nine-tenths of their income. The miller promised that he would pay all of the expenses of the church during the next year. He was paying most of the expenses anyway, and the people were delighted to hear that he would pay for everything. When the end of the year came, they thought it would be nice to show their appreciation for the tremendous amount of money given by the flour miller, so they gave a banquet in his honor.

Each member who had previously given grudgingly stood and spoke kind words of thanks. Finally, the miller in his response thanked them for the dinner and denied that he deserved any credit for either his generosity or helping the church financially. Neither could he receive their thanks and appreciation. He then explained that from each of their loads of grain they brought to the mill he had taken one-tenth and set it aside for God. Each one had really received pay for only nine-tenths of his grain. Not a single farmer present had missed the part that had been given to God. The miller concluded by saying, "I personally have been doing this for years in my own business, giving God a tenth. Never once have I missed God's tenth, and I knew that if I gave God a tenth of your increase, you would not miss it either."

The story, whether true or false, does not commend the miller's method. It does teach that anyone who desires can live on the part that is left after he or she gives the church what actually belongs to the Lord.

Tithing will continue until Jesus comes again. Tithing is God's plan and has the wisdom of omniscience and the power of omnipotence behind it. People may dislike tithing, they may complain about it, they may refuse to believe that it is God's plan, but tithing is certain for success. It is the will of God for every man, woman, boy, and girl to give a tenth of his or her increase to the work of God through the church.

Tithing is within the capacity of every Christian. If each of us would give to God that which is rightfully His, we could change the slow, mule pace of the Christian church into the speed of a jet supersonic airplane. We would create an atmosphere of success in the kingdom. We would relieve the poverty of the work of God and fulfill the Great Commission.

Columbus Roberts of Georgia felt this high calling in his life. At a banquet where he was being honored, it was stated that he had given thousands of dollars to Mercer University. At the banquet he told the story of his life. At eighteen he left the home farm in North Carolina and soon after made a profession of faith in Christ, joining a country church.

Roberts began to attend church and prayer meeting regularly. He felt that he could not take part in praying and testifying because of his lack of formal training. The thought came to him, "The church needs money, so I will live to help the church that way." His dedication to that need was as definite and holy as a youth making a commitment to be a foreign missionary. The gift to Mercer University was but one of his many beneficent gifts. He became Secretary of Agriculture for Georgia and a man of culture, refinement, and grace. Later the press reported that he had bequeathed the bulk of his estate to the Georgia Baptist Foundation, money that would support missionary work across that great state in coming generations.

Let us join with Columbus Roberts and determine that we will provide for the needs of God's church and kingdom. God promises that if we are faithful, He will open up the windows of heaven and pour us out a blessing. There are those who claim, and upon apparently good ground, that there is actually financial gain in tithing. I do not press this, but God is able to make it possible.

One deacon said that he and his wife were convicted that they ought to tithe when they barely were able to live on their income. No sooner had they decided to do it than the head of the business for which he worked called him in and said they were going to give him a raise. His boss also said that he had done such good work that he was to receive a bonus.

Would you join the great host of saints of the past who found tithing to be a blessing? Join hands with Abraham, Jacob, Moses, Malachi, Paul, and many of God's choice people in committing yourself to tithe. A Christian is one who is Christlike. The Bible teaches that Jesus tithed.

III. There Is a Mystery about the Method of Tithing

Why would God say that the tithe is the Lord's? God could have financed His church another way, if He had desired. Yet God has chosen to finance His church through the faithfulness of His people in tithing. The Bible explains the methodology of tithing.

First, God teaches us that we are to give one-tenth of our income to Him. Moses taught, "All the tithe of the land, . . . is holy unto the Lord" (Lev. 27:30). Malachi told the people that they were to bring all the tithes into the storehouse (3:10). We are clearly taught where our giving is to begin. It is to begin by giving one-tenth of our increase to God.

Second, we are to bring the first of our increase to God. The Bible teaches, "The first of the firstfruits of thy land thou shalt bring into the house of the Lord thy God" (Ex. 23:19). The writer of Proverbs reiterated this by saying, "Honour the Lord with thy substance, and with the firstfruits of all thine increase" (3:9). Notice that God did not tell us to wait until we had paid our debts to tithe. He does not tell us to wait until we are financially able to give. The person who waits until he or she has met all of his or her obligations is never able to tithe. God teaches that we are to give to Him first.

A. A. Hyde, a millionaire of Mentholatum manufacturing fame, said he began tithing when he was $100,000 in debt. Like others he had been warned that he should not tithe until he was out of debt. One day as he was reading the Bible, it dawned on him that "The earth is the Lord's, and the fulness thereof; the world, and they that dwell therein" (Ps. 24:1). That made God Hyde's first creditor. From that moment forward, he began paying God first, and, eventually, all of the other creditors were paid in full.

Third, God teaches us we are to give to Him on the first day of the week: Sunday. Paul taught the Corinthians, "Upon the first day of the week let every one of you lay by him in store, as God hath prospered him, that there be no gatherings when I come" (1 Cor. 16:2). The New Testament Christians assembled on Sunday. When they assembled, they were taught that they were to bring an offering to the Lord. The rule of thumb is that we are to give our tithes as soon as we make the money.

Fourth, the Bible teaches where we are to give our tithe. In the Old Testament, they brought the tithe to the temple. In the New Testament, we are to bring the tithe to the New Testament church where we are a member. The clear command of the Old Testament is, "Bring ye all the tithes into the storehouse" (Mal. 3:10). The apostle Paul said, "Let every one of you lay by him in store, . . . that there be no gatherings when I come" (1 Cor. 16:2). The principle is clear in the Old and New Testaments: people are to give their tithes to the church where they worship. The tithe was to be laid by in store in the Old Testament, and in the New Testament it was to be given in order that there would not have to be a continual special offering made for every need that arose. A church that is not worthy to receive and handle your tithe is not worthy of your membership.

IV. There Is a Mystery about the Material Results of Tithing

God promises to bless the tither: "Honour the Lord with thy substance, and with the firstfruits of all thine increase: So shall thy barns be filled with plenty, and thy presses shall burst out with new wine" (Prov. 3:9-10). When Paul wrote to the Corinthians, he said, "He which soweth sparingly shall reap also sparingly; and he which soweth bountifully shall reap also bountifully" (2 Cor. 9:6). Malachi said that if we will tithe, God will open the windows of heaven and pour us out a blessing that there will not be room enough to receive.

Jesus taught us that we're to lay up treasures in heaven. As a matter of fact, He taught in Luke 6:38, "Give, and it shall be given unto you; good measure, pressed down, and shaken together, and running over."

John D. Rockefeller, Sr., is reported to have given the following explanation as to how he came to know about tithing:

> Yes, I tithe, and I would like to tell you how it all came about. I had to begin work as a small boy to help support my mother. My first wages amounted to $1.50 per week. The first week after I went to work, I took the $1.50 home to my mother, and she held the money in her lap and explained to me that she would be happy if I would give one-tenth of it to the Lord. I did and from that week until this day, I have tithed every dollar God had entrusted to me. And I want to say to you, young men, if I had not tithed the first dollar I made, I would not have tithed the first million I made.[1]

Train the children to tithe, and they will grow up to be faithful stewards of the Lord.

V. There Is a Mystery about the Rejection of Tithing

Many people who are Christians today refuse to tithe. This is extremely difficult to understand. How can we receive all the blessings that God pours out on us so abundantly and yet refuse to obey the clear teaching of the Bible regarding tithing. Tithing is God's plan. It is a biblical plan. It is a plan practiced by Jesus.

Years ago a lad of sixteen left home to seek his fortune. All of his worldly possessions were tied in a bundle that he carried in his hand. As he trudged along, he met an old neighbor, the captain of a canal boat. The following conversation took place, which changed the boy's life:

"Well, William, where are you going?"

"I don't know," he answered. "Father is too poor to keep me at home any longer and says that I must now make a living for myself."

"There's no trouble about that," said the captain. "Be sure you start right, and you'll get along fine."

William told his friend that the only trade he could do was soap and candle making. He had helped his father do both while at home. "Well," said the old man, "let me pray with you once more and give you a little advice, and then I will let you go." They both knelt down on the tow path, and the dear old man prayed earnestly for William and then gave him this advice, "Someone will soon be the leading soap maker in New York. It can be you as well as anyone. I hope it may. Be a good man; give your heart to Christ; give the Lord all that belongs to Him of every dollar you earn; make an honest soap, give a full pound, and I am certain that yet you will be a prosperous and a rich man."

When the boy arrived in New York City, he found it hard to get work. Lonesome and far from home, he remembered the last words of the canal captain. He was then led to "Seek . . . first the kingdom of God, and his righteousness" and united with the church. He remembered his promise to the old captain, and the first dollar he earned brought up the question of the Lord's part: *I will give one-tenth of my income.* So he did, and ten cents of every dollar was sacred to the Lord.

He soon became a partner, and after a few years when the other partner died, William became the sole owner of the business. He had resolved to keep his promise to the old captain, so he made an honest soap, gave a full pound, and instructed his bookkeeper to open an account with the Lord, carrying 10 percent of his income to the account. He prospered. His business grew. His family was blessed. His soap sold. He grew rich faster than he had ever hoped. He began to give the Lord two-tenths, and he prospered even more. Then he gave God three-tenths and four-tenths and, finally, fifty percent of everything he made. He educated his family, settled all of his plans for life, and thereafter gave one hundred percent of his income to the Lord.[2]

Who was this young man that became so fabulously successful? His name was William Colgate. He was the founder of the Colgate Palmolive soap and toothpaste enterprises. He recognized himself as a steward of God and experienced the joy of the mystery of tithing.

You and I have the gospel of Jesus Christ. There are hungry hearts and souls the world over that are longing to hear the message of God. It is ours to keep or to give. It is ours to send or to share with others. By the marvelous alchemy of God's blessings, our dollars are turned into gospel messages. When you and I give our tithes on the Lord's Day to the Lord's church, for the Lord's work, we are taking the Lord's gospel to the ends of the earth. Nothing could be more joyful than that—sharing in the mystery of tithing.

    1. Walter B. Knight, *Knight's Master Book of New Illustrations* (Grand Rapids, Mich.: Wm. B. Eerdmans, 1956), 689.
    2. Knight, *Three Thousand Illustrations*, 696.

12
Lift Up Your Eyes

(Matt. 9:35-38)

Bill Sands lived in the biggest house on the highest hill in Whittier, California. His father was a distinguished judge. His mother was a prominent socialite. Seemingly, the environment of his home was perfect.

About 2:00 a.m., Bill was awakened by his mother. She said, "Your father and I want you to talk with us in the living room." Half asleep, the twelve-year-old boy was led into the formal living area where his father was sitting in a high wing-backed chair. Looking at Bill, and with no apparent emotion, his mother said, "Bill, your dad and I are going to divorce. We want you to tell us with which one of us you would like to live."

Neither parent said, "I love you," or, "I want you," nor did either give any explanation. Bill's whole world came crashing down. He began to cry and ran back up to his room.

In a few moments, Bill's mother was back in his bedroom. She took him by the hand and unemotionally led him into the living area once again. "Bill, a boy's place is with his mother. You'll live with me." The next day, the father moved out of the house.

A year later, a little after five in the afternoon, Bill arrived home from school. His mother was working with the rose bushes that climbed up the front of their two-story house. She did not speak to him. That was not too unusual. Bill went up to his room and began to wash his face, having removed his shirt. Suddenly, he was aware that his mother was behind him. She inquired, "Why were you late?" Before he could respond, she said, "I will teach you never to be late again."

Before Bill could answer, his back began to ache with pain. His mother had taken the rose bushes with their quarter-of-an-inch thorns, wrapped them in the form of a whip, and used them to lacerate his back. When the beating finally stopped, his aching back was set aflame with pain as his mother sloshed alcohol on his open wounds. Bill fainted and fell to the floor.

During the next years of Bill's life, he made straight A's in school; he was on the basketball team and served as editor of the school newspaper, but he received very little commendation. His mother seemed to be extremely critical, and every letter that his father sent was intercepted.

By the time Bill Sands was twenty years of age, his name had been changed. Instead of a name, he had a number—66836. He was a life termer in San Quentin penitentiary.

A new inmate came into the penitentiary. When he saw Bill Sands, he asked, "Isn't your dad a judge?"

Bill responded, "Yes."

The new inmate's eyes flashed with rage and anger, "Your dad sentenced my brother to the penitentiary. When I get out of here, I am going to kill him." Like a wild animal, Bill pounced on the man, smashing his head into the floor. He would have killed the new inmate, except two guards intervened.

That night Bill found himself in a room four-and-a-half feet by ten feet. His meals consisted mainly of bread and water. Days turned into weeks, and weeks turned into months. Bill thought he would lose his mind.

One day the door of that solitary confinement cell swung open. Facing Bill was a short man, Clinton T. Duffy, warden of San Quentin penitentiary.

"Bill, may I come in?" Rather astonished, Bill beckoned the warden into his cell. Warden Duffy said, "Bill, that young man is going to live, no thanks to you. But, I've come to ask you: Why are you here in the first place? Your IQ indicates you are nearly a genius. I don't understand why you act like you do. Why are you here?"

Filling the room with profanity, Bill responded: "Because no one cares for me." In his marvelous book, *My Shadow Ran Fast*, Bill wrote, "My whole life was turned around with just three words as the warden said, 'Bill, I care.'"

"No one cares for me" is the statement that many people in our world are saying. Hundreds of years ago, the psalmist wrote, "No man cared for my soul" (142:4). That is the attitude of many in our world today. Against that backdrop, God sent His Son Jesus to journey from heaven down to earth to show us that God really cares. God in heaven is vitally concerned about you.

If someone were to ask me to summarize the whole ministry of our Lord in one word, I would use the word *compassion*. This is a word of Latin origin, coming from *com*, meaning "with" and *passion*, meaning "to suffer." Our redeeming Savior suffers with us. As a matter of fact, He was tempted in all points as we are, yet He was without sin. He knew what it was to be hungry, weary, thirsty, tired, and even angry. He even comprehends what it is like to die, having died for our sins on the cross of Calvary.

The Gospel of Matthew records that when Jesus saw the multitudes, He was moved with compassion because they were like sheep with no shepherd. They were like a field white unto harvest with no reapers. That describes the desperate condition of our world today. The word *fainted* has reference to a corpse that is laying by the side of the road, flayed and mangled (Matt. 9:36). The phrase "scattered abroad" means to lay prostrate with deep, mortal wounds (Matt. 9:36). This is the way men and women are apart from God.

When Jesus saw the multitudes in this desperate condition, He encouraged His disciples to lift up their eyes, saying that the fields were white unto harvest. "The harvest truly is plenteous, but the labourers are few; Pray ye therefore the Lord of the harvest, that he will send forth labourers into his harvest" (v. 37).

This is the pressing need of the church today. You and I as Christ's church need to lift up our eyes to the desperate spiritual condition of men and women, boys and girls in our world today.

I. The Waiting Harvest

When the Pharisees looked at people, all they could think of was that they were contemptible sinners. On the other hand, when Jesus saw the crowd, He saw them as sheep who had no shepherd. The unregenerate are not able to quote the beautiful twenty-third Psalm with any form of assurance. The Lord has never really become their Shepherd.

One of the greatest things the church of the Lord Jesus Christ can do is to reexamine its purpose for existence. Jesus never saw a hungry man that He did not want to feed. He never saw anyone who was sad that He did not want to comfort. He never saw a lonely person that He did not want to befriend. He never saw a sick man that He did not want to heal, and He never saw a sinner that He did not want to save. The church could do and is doing many wonderful things, but we must ask ourselves, "What is the church's chief purpose for existing?" The chief purpose of the church of Jesus Christ is redemption.

A. A Christlike Compassion

When our Lord saw the multitudes, He was moved with compassion. He did not see them as they were, but He saw what they could become. We must look at the world through the eyes of our Savior.

When Jesus saw Matthew, He did not see a conniving, cheating, and thieving politician. Rather, He saw the writer of the first Gospel. When Jesus met Simon Peter, He wasn't looking at a cursing fisherman. He was anticipating the day that Peter would be the great preacher of Pentecost. When a woman taken in adultery was brought to Christ, He did not see her as a harlot; He saw a potential home missionary. And when Jesus saw Saul of Tarsus persecuting the church, He did not see a cruel persecutor; He saw the greatest missionary the world would ever know, the apostle Paul. Christian history shows that the worst sinners can become the greatest saints. You and I are to reach out with an arm of love to bring them to our Savior.

Several years ago, a seventy-year-old man named Robert came to my office. Barging in, he said, "I want to talk to you for a minute." When I asked him to sit down, he said, "I don't want to sit down."

Robert said: "I've operated a liquor store all of my life. I've quit the liquor business, but my heart is not right with God. Could you tell me how to become a Christian?"

I answered, "Yes sir, I can." Opening the Bible, I began to share the love of God through faith in Jesus Christ. As I presented the plan of salvation, the man began to weep. We got down on our knees, and Robert gave his heart to Jesus Christ. The next Sunday, he joined the church, and the following Sunday, he was baptized. In the providence of God, he lived well into his eighties. Nearly every month, he would walk with someone down the aisle, leading them to Christ. The last decade of his life, he was one of the greatest soul-winners I have ever known. He had a Christlike compassion. That is the compassion you and I need—the compassion of the Savior. When Jesus saw the multitudes, He began to weep and encouraged us to lift up our eyes to the fields that are ripe for harvesting.

B. A Christlike Commission

As we see the world, we will not only have a Christlike compassion, but I think we will also have a Christlike commission. The purpose of our ministry must be clear. There are many members in churches today that do not have a clear understanding of what they are to do. You and I are to be about the business of winning people to Christ, baptizing them, and teaching them to observe all things that Christ has commanded (Matt. 28:19-20).

Jesus taught us that people need to be reached, for the Bible states, "Jesus went about all the cities and villages." People need to be taught. Matthew tells us that Jesus was "teaching in their synagogues." People need to hear preaching. The Bible states that Jesus was "preaching the gospel of the kingdom." People need healing. As Jesus reached people, taught people, and preached to people, He ultimately healed them. Matthew tells us that Jesus went about "healing every sickness and every disease among the people" (Matt. 9:35).

The church is to evangelize people, enlist, and enlighten people (Matt. 28:19-20). When our Lord won Zacchaeus, He summarized His whole ministry in one sentence: "The Son of man is come to seek and to save that which was lost" (Luke 19:19). In the final business meeting with the church before Jesus ascended to the right hand of the Father in heaven, there was only one item on the agenda: evangelism and world missions. John Wesley, founder of the Methodist Church, said, "The only business that you have, young ministers, is the salvation of souls." Professor Schmearton of Edinburgh University, who long since has gone to be with the Lord, stated, "Gentlemen, reckon your ministry a failure if you do not win souls to the Lord Jesus Christ."

Margaret Sangster, the great social worker, related a story that indicates her patience, compassion, and love. As she worked in a gymnasium in a metropolitan city, a boy came hobbling in on two crutches. His feet were turned in almost facing each other. Sangster's heart went out to him.

One day she inquired, "Have you ever gone to a doctor to see if you can be helped?"

The lad responded, "My parents are so poor that we have never even talked about that."

With the permission of the boy's parents, Sangster took the lad to an orthopedic surgeon. The findings were encouraging. The surgeon said, "Margaret, with a series of five operations that will take a period of two years of convalescence, I can have that boy walking and running." The doctor offered his services without cost. A local banker raised the money to pay the hospital bill and incidental expenses. The five operations were performed, and some two years later, the boy came back into the gymnasium.

Sangster said, "I was in the gym the day that the young boy came back. He picked up a basketball, dribbled it down the court and leaping off his feet, he placed it in the basket. My heart nearly jumped out of my breast I was so excited. I said to myself, 'There is one boy that I have helped.'"

But, as Margaret related the story, her voice trembled. She asked the crowd: "Do you know where that boy is today? I wish I could tell you that he is a teacher, carpenter, an electrician, a doctor, a lawyer, a preacher, or governmental employee. Unfortunately, he is none of these. In fact, he is in the penitentiary. He murdered seventeen people!" Then Margaret Sangster said with great insight, "I was so busy teaching that boy *how* to walk that I forgot to teach him *where* to walk." It is ever the job of the church to point people to Christ and to say to them, "This is the way, walk ye in it" (Isa. 30:21).

II. The Necessity of Enlisting the Layperson

Jesus knew that the success of His church was dependent on enlisting the layperson. He chose twelve disciples as He began His ministry, and there was not a single priest or Levite in the group.

When Jesus told His disciples that the laborers were few, they must have been shocked. The priests in Jerusalem were so numerous in Jesus' day that they had to take turns in performing temple ceremonies. There were twelve tribes in Israel, one of which was the tribe of Levi. Every member of that tribe was dedicated to religious service. In the face of this, Jesus shocked His disciples by saying, "The labourers are few." The temple dominated the landscape in Jerusalem, yet Jesus said the laborers were few. There were many synagogues, and yet Jesus said the laborers were few. Religion was the biggest business in Israel, and yet Jesus said the laborers were few.

If the world is ever going to be won to Christ, it must be won by the laypeople of the church. Jesus said that we need to pray for laborers. The difficulty of the church today is that Christianity has become too professional. We have a "let-the-preacher-do-it" syndrome. We must ever remember that all Christians are in full-time Christian service. The minister works at the church. The laypeople work outside the church, but they, too, are in full-time Christian service.

A man was asked, "What is your occupation?"

"Being a Christian."

"No, what's your chief interest?"

"Being a Christian."

"No, what is your business?"

"Winning people to Christ. I work at my job to pay expenses."

That must ever be the attitude of every member of Christ's church.

Satan's strategy in our world today is to convince the laypeople of the church that Christianity is complicated, winning people to

Christ is too complex, and only ministers can do it. What if someone could convince us that wars are too complicated, dangerous, and only generals can fight wars?

You and I are to penetrate the society in which we live with the gospel of Jesus Christ. The Great Commission begins with the phrase, "[As you are going,] make disciples" (Matt. 28:19, RSV).

A lady disembarked from an airplane after talking with a handsome man. Her jealous husband asked, "What did you talk with that man about?"

"Nothing in particular, but he asked the strangest question, 'Are you a Christian?'"

The husband responded, "Why didn't you tell him it was none of his business?"

Hugging her husband she said, "Had you heard him speak, you would have known that it *was* his business."

That is the spirit you and I must have as we share the gospel of Christ in the world in which we live. We need to be like the elevator operator who would say to people in the elevator, "Make sure your last trip is up." We must never be contented as keepers of the aquarium when Jesus has commanded us to be fishers of men.

III. The Urgency of the Task

One of the great secrets of Jesus' ministry and success was His comprehension of the urgency of the task. Listen to Jesus, "Lift up your eyes . . . the fields . . . are white already to harvest" (John 4:35). When the fields are white, they must be harvested immediately, or they are lost. Normally, the farmers reap the fields when they are yellow unto harvest, not white.

As Jesus looked out at lost humanity, He saw them perishing as sheep with no shepherd, as a field ready to be reaped with no harvester. That is a picture of our world today.

According to the 1987 world population sheet, there were in 1986:

- 4.4 births per second
- 265 births per minute
- 15,879 births per hour
- 381,101 births per day

- 2,675,035 births per week
- 11,591,817 births per month
- 139,101,802 births per year

Every year there are 139 million new people born into the world. All churches of all denominations under the Christian umbrella win less than five million of these people a year to Jesus Christ. We must aggressively seek out those who are unsaved and do our utmost to lead them to our Savior.

The Bible in every one of more than eleven hundred editions says "come" six hundred times. Let us not go about in this world saying, "Look what the world has come to." Instead, let us say, "Look who has come to the world!"

13
The House of God

(Gen. 28:10-22)

Jacob's dream at Bethel is one of the loveliest events in the Bible. Poets, painters, hymn writers, and preachers all have paused at Bethel, trying to interpret exactly what happened to Jacob. He was a young man who needed the presence of God. Just when he needed God the most—lonely, frightened, homesick, smitten of conscience, and facing an uncertain future—God appeared to him and was right by his side.

Jacob's meeting God in his hour of greatest need has become an experience that we have shared with him. Jacob realized that God is merciful and forgiving. He discovered through faith and obedience to God that God would bless and care for him wherever he went. When Jacob met God, he called the name of the place Bethel, meaning this is "the house of God."

Probably all of us have had or shall have one experience in life when God seems nearer to us than He has been at any other time. It may be some hour of sorrow or joy. It may be at a church or on a lake. It may be when some marvelous thing happened to you, or it may be when you are in the hospital facing surgery. The experience of God's nearness may be in a moment of supreme joy like a marriage, or in a moment of deep sorrow by a graveside at a funeral. Whatever the time, place, or hour, we can always say of it, "This is the gate of heaven; this is the house of God."

What is the house of God? In the United States and Canada there are over 300,000 Protestant churches, thousands of Catholic churches, and hundreds of other worship centers. Every one is called "the house of God." What does this passage from Genesis teach about the house of God?

Isaac, the father of Jacob, sent Jacob away from home so that he could find a wife. It was the desire of Jacob's father that his son marry a young lady who believed in God as deeply as Abraham, Jacob's grandfather. Marriages are stronger when both the husband and wife have a belief in the living God and a commitment to God's house.

Jacob went down toward Haran. Perhaps this was the first night he had ever spent away from home. He was very lonely. Jacob found a place that seemed to be comfortable and camped out with the stars as his roof. While he was asleep, he had a marvelous dream. Heaven opened, and he saw a ladder set up on the earth reaching into heaven. He was conscious of movement between earth and heaven. He saw the angels of God ascending into heaven and descending back to earth. When Jacob awakened, he said, "This is the house of God. I've seen God here." As he said that, God spoke to him, saying: "Jacob, I'm here by your side; and if you will be faithful to me, I will go with you wherever you go and I will multiply your descendants. You will become a wealthy man, and through your children many people will 'be blessed.'"

Jacob became so excited about this dream and God speaking to him that he took the stones that he had used for a pillow and put them in a great heap. He poured oil on them and said, "This is none other but the house of God"! What is the house of God?

I. The House of God Is a Place Where Our Vision Is Enlarged

When we come to the house of God to worship, we ought to have our vision enlarged. The church is the place where we are to dream without falling asleep. As we assemble to worship God, we ought to dream of what God would have us to accomplish in this world.

James Russell Lowell has described the effect that Emerson had on young people in his day. He said that after hearing Emerson they went out not entirely sure what he had said, but with their heads "hitting the stars."

Jacob had this experience. The Bible states: "He dreamed, and behold a ladder set up on the earth, and the top of it reached to heaven: and behold the angels of God ascending and descending on it" (Gen. 28:12). Jacob's vision at Bethel was a life-transforming experience. He would never be the same.

What happened to the great men and women in the Bible when they went to church? They went out with a new vision. Young Isaiah, the student, went to the temple, and in the temple he saw the Lord high and lifted up. The magnificence of God was so great that his life was never the same. He cried out, "Here am I; send me" (6:8).

When Peter, James, and John saw Jesus transfigured, the Bible states their vision was lifted, and they said, "Let us make here three tabernacles" (Matt. 17:4). When John, the beloved disciple, was banished to the isle of Patmos, on the Lord's Day he received a vision as he worshiped. He saw into eternity. God gave him a view of a new heaven and a new earth where the kingdoms of this world became the kingdom of our Lord and where Jesus reigns forever and ever.

The house of God ought to teach us to be positive, dynamic, and believing. Jesus said, "Blessed are they that have not seen, and yet have believed" (John 20:29). How important that is! When we come to the house of God, our visions ought to be lifted, our spirits ought to be enlarged, and the horizons of our faith lengthened.

A noted artist was working on great mural. He intended for it to be a masterpiece. A friend came into the studio and stood quietly in the rear of the room, looking at the work as the artist slapped on the deep blue and gray tones across the canvas for the background. Wishing to view the work from a better perspective, he descended the ladder and backed right into his friend without seeing him. Enthusiastically the artist said: "This is going to be the masterpiece of my life! What do you think of it?"

His friend replied, "All that I see is a great, dull dob."

The artist responded: "Oh, I forgot. When you look at the painting, you see only what it is. When I look at it, I see what it is going to be!"

That's the difference in people in the world today. The great thing about going to church is that the church lifts our vision from earth to heaven. The church lifts our vision from the here to the hereafter. The church lifts our vision from now to the future. When we come to the house of God, we see beyond conflict and war to permanent peace. When we come to the house of God in the midst of our struggles, we see that victory is ours. The house of God lifts our sight from time into eternity. In the house of God our vision is lifted.

II. The House of God Is a Place Where People Are Pointed to Heaven

When Jacob had his vision at Bethel, he found himself pointed to heaven. "He dreamed, and behold a ladder set up on the earth, and the top of it reached to heaven: and behold the angels of God ascending and descending on it" (Gen. 28:12). That is what Jacob saw. He saw heaven: "He was afraid, and said, How dreadful is this place! this is none other but the house of God, and this is the gate of heaven" (v. 17).

That is what the church is about. The church is the house of God that points men and women to heaven. The church is like a ladder that leads people from earth to heaven. The church is the finger of God pointing men and women to eternity. That is the main task of the church, to point people to heaven.

Michelangelo, the great artist and sculptor, lingered before a rough rock of marble. As he stared at the stone block, one of his students asked, "What are you doing?"

Michelangelo responded, "I'm looking at this block of marble. There is an angel in it, and I'm going to liberate him!" That is what the church is doing. We see a man or woman who is down and out and say: "There is an angel in you. You realize you are a sinner. God wants you to be a saint. Inside of you there is a part of God Himself." The church is in the business of pointing men and women to heaven to bring out the best.

III. The House of God Is a Place Where the Promises of God Are Repeated

One of the wonderful things about coming to church is that in church we hear the promises of God repeated. That was Jacob's experience at Bethel: "Behold, the Lord stood above it, and said, I am the Lord God of Abraham thy father, and the God of Isaac: the land whereon thou liest, to thee will I give it, and to thy seed" (Gen. 28:13).

Studying this passage carefully we notice that in Genesis 28:12 there is evangelism, and in verse 13 there is discipleship. In the church through evangelism we are taught how to become a Christian. Then the church disciples us, teaching us how to be a growing Christian. That was Jacob's experience.

The church must always major in evangelism. It is said of Jacob, "He dreamed, and behold a ladder set up on the earth, and the top of it reached to heaven" (v. 12). The church indeed is to be used of God, showing people the ladder that leads them to heaven. Jesus said, "I am the way, the truth, and the life: no man cometh unto the Father, but by me" (John 14:6). Peter preached, "There is none other name under heaven given among men, whereby we must be saved" (Acts 4:12).

But when a person becomes a Christian, that is not the end of the pilgrimage. The Bible tells us that we are to grow in grace and in the knowledge of our Lord and Savior Jesus Christ. That was Jacob's experience, for the next verse states, "Behold, the Lord stood above it, and said, I am the Lord God of Abraham thy father, and the God of Isaac: the land whereon thou liest, to thee will I give it, and to thy seed" (Gen. 28:13). Here we find teaching, as God instructed Jacob on what took place in the past and what would take place in the future. He also was promising He would be with Jacob.

Evangelism tells us how to become a Christian. Then we are taught how to be a good Christian. When Paul wrote to the young preacher Titus, he stated, "The grace of God that bringeth salvation hath appeared to all men" (2:11). That is evangelism through the grace of God. Paul went on instructing Titus, "Teaching us that, denying ungodliness and worldly lusts, we should live soberly, righteously, and godly, in this present world" (v. 12).

Jacob had that experience at Bethel as he heard the promises of God repeated. There are many rich promises in the Word of God.

Jesus promises His presence, "Lo, I am with you always." God promises to meet our need, "My God shall supply all your need according to his riches in glory by Christ Jesus." God promised to forgive our sins, "If we confess our sins, he is faithful and just to forgive us our sins, and to cleanse us from all unrighteousness." God promises us strength, saying, "As thy days, so shall thy strength be." God promises to answer our prayer, "Call upon me in the day of trouble: I will deliver thee, and thou shalt glorify me." And God promises to take everything and work it together for good in Romans 8:28.

When we come to the house of God, the promises of God are reaffirmed in our lives. We are given courage to face whatever tomorrow brings.

IV. The House of God Is a Place Where God's Presence Is Felt

God said to Jacob, "I am with thee, and will keep thee in all places whether thou goest, and will bring thee again into this land; for I will not leave thee, until I have done that which I have spoken to thee of" (Gen. 28:15). Hearing that, Jacob built an altar and poured oil on the rock, for Jacob had experienced the presence of the living God. In the Bible, oil is a symbol of the Holy Spirit. Just as Jacob poured oil on the rock, so the living God had come to be present with Jacob. When we come to the house of God, one of the great things that happens to us is that we experience the presence of God.

Have you ever been in church and as a song was being sung felt the presence of the Holy Spirit? Have you ever been in church and the minister quoted a Scripture or gave some illustration out of the Bible that lifted your heart and soul toward the Father? Have you ever been in a prayer meeting where you knew Jesus was there, and He was speaking to your heart? That's what happens when we come to the house of God—we feel God's presence.

A young man one day asked Christ what is the greatest commandment. Jesus responded that we are to love God with all of our hearts, souls, minds, and strength (Mark 12:30). Jesus said that we are to love God first emotionally "with all" of our heart. Then we are to love Him spiritually with our souls. Then we are to love Him intellectually with our minds. Then we are to love God practically with our strength. But loving God begins in our hearts, emotionally, as we feel His presence.

You and I need to get excited about our faith. We need to get enthused about the matter of serving Jesus Christ. Church is a place where we feel the presence of the Lord.

Some men in Ireland were watching a parade. The Christian flag passed in front of them and one said, "Let's give three cheers for God and the church." As the Christian flag passed by, they said, "Praise the Lord! Praise the Lord! Praise the Lord!"

An infidel standing by them laughed and said, "Why don't you give three cheers for hell?" The Christian Irishman looked at him and responded, "Every man ought to be for his own country." We are excited about Christ and the church. We exclaim, "Praise the Lord! The house of God is a place where God's presence is felt."

V. The House of God Is a Place Where Vows Are Made

At Bethel, Jacob vowed a vow to God. That is certainly an important part of coming to the house of God. Jacob's vow is one that each of us should consider making: "Jacob vowed a vow, saying, If God will be with me, and will keep me in this way that I go, and will give me bread to eat, and raiment to put on, so that I come again to my Father's house in peace; then shall the Lord be my God: and this stone, which I have set for a pillar, shall be God's house: and of all that thou shalt give me I will surely give the tenth unto thee" (Gen. 28:20-22).

In many of our churches, this passage of Scripture reinforces the importance of calling for a response to the gospel. In a sense the most important moment in any service comes when the invitation is extended for people to come and make definite commitments to God. That is the time when every one of us ought to be praying regarding what God would have us to do. During those moments, souls are moved to trust Christ as Savior. People come to unite with the church. Others rededicate their lives in repentance to God. During the invitation, many people who do not come forward publicly do make vows privately in their hearts. That's what the church is supposed to be, a place where you and I make vows to God.

When you come to church, do you make vows to God? It is important that we tell God what we intend to do. I think it is critical we commit to God that we will seek to do certain things to honor His name. Jacob made a very important vow. He promised he would show his love for God by tithing (Gen. 28:22). Do you tithe?

Actually, when people tithe, what they are doing is giving a part of themselves to God. A tithe represents one tenth of our increase or income. That means that every time we work ten minutes, we have given one of those minutes to God. Every time we work ten days, we have given one of those days to God. This means that God is a vital part of everything we do.

VI. The House of God Helps People Face the Future

Perhaps the most striking thing about the house of God is that it is a place that helps people face the future with great confidence and courage. The Bible tells us that as Jacob went out, he was afraid. As he first began to get this vision of God, he said, "How dreadful is this place!" But after God spoke to him, he saw heaven and the angels; he made a vow in his heart to God; he built an altar, and he said, "This is a sacred place." Jacob realized that this was the most wonderful thing that ever happened to him. Verse 3 relates, "Behold, the Lord stood above it." You see, in the house of God we get the courage that we need to face the future with total confidence because we know that the Lord is with us.

God said, "I'll be your God, Jacob." Jacob responded, "I'll be your servant, God." That's what worship is all about. We come to the house of God, we commit ourselves to the Lord, we realize that God is with us, and we are able to face the future with confidence.

A partially crippled young man had to wear steel braces on his legs. Often, he and his father would talk about his crippled condition. When the young man reached the age of thirteen, he began to ask his dad, "Why am I partially crippled?" The father, a devout believer, tried to explain it but didn't have much success.

One day the boy asked again, "Why do I have this crippled condition?" The father laid his hand on the shoulder of his son and said: "God's going to deal with you. I am going to take you to the great cathedral, and God is going to heal you."

Following that, the boy often would ask his father, "When are we going to the cathedral so I can be healed?" The response was, "It's not time yet."

After a year, the father said: "Son, it's time. We're going to the cathedral, and you are going to be healed."

The boy related, "I was so excited I could hardly stand it. My father and I went to the great cathedral. We were the only ones there. We went to the back of the church, got down on our knees, and my father said, 'Now, Son, pray. God is going to heal you.'"

The boy said, "My father laid his arm around me and prayed. I could feel the power of God." As the father prayed, the boy said, "I knew that I was healed. After a long while in prayer, my father and I got up and walked out of the cathedral together. After we had gone almost two blocks on the way home I realized I still had those braces on my legs. I hadn't been physically healed." But the boy said, "All of the sudden I realized that I really had been healed because in that cathedral God had taken the braces off my mind, and that's where they were doing me damage, not the ones on my legs. From that day forth, I knew that I had been healed and freed, though I still had the braces."

That's what the church does for us. Sometimes God heals us, but sometimes He takes the braces off our minds with the freedom of the faith that can trust God. That is what happened to Jacob. He was never the same. Jacob caught a view of the future, and he could face it with confidence. He said, "The Lord is in this place" (v. 16). The Bible says that the Lord God stood above the place to watch over Jacob. That's what happens when we come to the house of God. We get the strength in our hearts to face the future with courage and confidence.

14
Melt Down the Saints

(1 Thess. 1:1-3)

During the reign of Oliver Cromwell in England, the government ran out of silver coinage. Cromwell sent his ministers throughout England to find new sources of silver. When they returned, the ministers reported that there was no silver to be found in England except in the statues of the saints in the churches. Cromwell said, "Then we'll melt down the saints and put them into circulation."

Many saints today need to be melted down and put into circulation. Some who are children of God are not very active in the work of the Lord God. They could well stand to be melted by the fire of the Holy Spirit and be used in a more dynamic way.

The third most frequently used word in the New Testament to designate the Christian is the word *saint*. A saint is not some figure in a stained glass window; a saint is anyone who by faith has received Jesus Christ as Lord and Savior. In the Old Testament the word *saint* is used thirty-nine times to denote the people of Israel. In the New Testament the word *saint* is used sixty-two times to designate believers in Jesus Christ. All who have received Christ as Savior are saints of God.

When Paul wrote to the church at Thessalonica, he addressed a church where the saints had been melted down and put into circulation. He discussed the wonderful character of this particular church in the opening verses of 1 Thessalonians.

Character is different from reputation. Reputation is what people think you are. Character is what you really are. Webster wrote, "Character is made up of those qualities and attributes that make a man what he is." Dwight L. Moody said, "Character is what you are in the dark." There is no substitute for good character.

When Stanley Baldwin was elected prime minister of Great Britain, a disgruntled politician in Parliament said, "Too bad, he has a second-class mind." Overhearing that statement, a friend of Baldwin replied, "That may be true, but he has a first-class character." It is better to have a first-class character and a second-class mind than to have a first-class mind and a second-class character.

Just as people have character, so churches have character. Because a church is an aggregate of many people, every church takes on the character and characteristics of its membership. Some churches are aggressive. Some are timid. Some churches are very rich. They minister to the wealthy. Others are very poor. Some churches look backward. They always talk about the history of the good old days. Some churches look forward. They discuss what is going to be done tomorrow. Some churches preach only a social gospel and seek to alleviate the physical ills of humankind. Other churches preach a gospel of redemption through faith in Jesus Christ.

The church at Thessalonica had discernible character traits. Paul summarized the character of this church in three words. These three words also described the graces that all of us need in our character. He said the brethren had faith, love, and hope. He talked about their work of faith, their labor of love, and their patience of hope.

This triad of Christian graces is mentioned often by the apostle Paul. For example, he addressed himself to the church at Colossae: "We heard of your faith in Christ Jesus, and of the love which ye have to all the saints, for the hope which is laid up for you in heaven" (Col. 1:4-5). To the Galatians he wrote, "We through the Spirit wait for the hope of righteousness by faith . . . faith which worketh by love" (Gal. 5:5-6). And he wrote to the Corinthians, "Now abideth faith, hope, [love], these three; but the greatest of these is [love]" (1 Cor. 13:13).

As Paul discussed the character of the church and used these three words—faith, love, and hope—he also was discussing the tenses of the Christian life. He talked about how believers become

Christians, how they progress in the Christian faith, and how ultimately they will be with Jesus Christ.

Look at Thessalonians 1 and compare verse 3 with verses 9 and 10. He talked about their work of faith in verse 3. In verse 9 he said that they turned to God from idols. He talked about their labor of love in verse 3, and in verse 9 he said that they served the living and true God. In verse 3 he said that they have patience of hope. In verse 10 he said that they waited for the Son from heaven, whom God raised from the dead, even Jesus.

These three words—faith, love, and hope—tell us how the believer turns from idols, serves God, and waits for the coming of Jesus Christ. These are the three stages of development in the Christian life. Faith rests on the past. Love labors in the present. Hope looks to the future. The believer is justified by faith, sanctified by love, and will be glorified by hope.

Paul was speaking of the very heart of the redemptive process of God. As he discussed faith, love, and hope, he told how they operate. Faith works. Love goes beyond that and labors. Hope, on the other hand, develops tremendous patience. In 1 Thessalonians 1:1-3 Paul summarized the character of the Christian church as it was in the ancient day and as it should be today.

I. A Faith That Works

Melt down the saints and put them in circulation because Christians need a faith that works. What is faith? The writer of Hebrews said, "Now faith is the substance of things hoped for, the evidence of things not seen" (Heb. 11:1). The word *substance* means "substantiating," and the word *evidence* means "conviction." So faith is the substantiating of things hoped for and the conviction of things not seen. Faith says, "God, I want it. I have it. Thank you." Faith rests on the promise of God.

At least three different kinds of faith are mentioned in the New Testament. The first is an intellectual or historical faith. It is a mental exercise whereby a person says, "I believe a certain thing." It does not necessarily affect the life. Many people give a mere intellectual assent to the credentials of Christianity.

Of this faith the Bible says, "Thou believest that there is one God; thou doest well: the devils also believe, and tremble" (Jas. 2:19). The demons that serve Satan have an intellectual faith. They give assent that God is God. But they do nothing about it. They are damned as a consequence.

The second kind of faith is emotional. An evangelist sometimes can work up this kind of faith in people by getting them to doubt their salvation; by lifting them up, hanging them over the pit of hell, and shaking them hard; or by telling a tear-jerking story. People's consciences are stirred, and their emotions are touched.

Jesus discussed this faith in Matthew 13:6. He said that some people receive the Word of God with great joy; but because there is no depth (their faith is emotional and shallow) when the fire of trial comes, that which has sprung up withers away and dies. There is nothing left. Many who have dropped out of the ranks of the church have dropped out because their faith was only emotional.

The third kind of faith is a volitional faith, a faith of conviction. It is a living, saving, dynamic, and life-changing faith. It is the kind of faith that Paul attributed to the Thessalonians when he wrote, "I think of the work of your faith." You can tell when an individual has saving faith because saving faith always produces good works.

An interesting balance exists in the Bible between works and faith. In Ephesians 2:8-10, within the confines of three verses of Scripture, Paul condemned trusting in works and then in the same breath commended good works. In verses 8-9 the apostle wrote, "For by grace are ye saved through faith; and that not of yourselves: it is the gift of God: Not of works, lest any man should boast." But in verse 10 he said, "For we are his workmanship, created in Christ Jesus unto good works."

There are the two sides of the Christian faith. Works before salvation are nothing. But after a person expresses faith in Christ and becomes a Christian, he or she lives and thrives on his or her works for the Lord Jesus Christ.

Writing to the church at Rome, Paul said, "Abraham believed God, and it was counted unto him for righteousness" (Rom. 4:3). James spoke of the faith of Abraham and then said, "Was not Abraham our father justified by works, when he had offered Isaac his son upon the altar?" (Jas. 2:21).

Do they contradict each other? No, because they refer to two different experiences. Paul said Abraham was justified by faith when he was called originally and left Ur of the Chaldees. He was speaking of the conversion of Abraham. James, on the other hand, said Abraham was justified by works when he offered up Isaac. He was speaking of something that happened years later, long after he had become a child of God.

The natural outgrowth of faith is works, and James and Paul were in agreement. Paul was talking about how God sees faith, and James was talking about how people see works. Paul was talking about the root of religion: faith. James was talking about the fruit of religion: works.

When Paul wrote to the church at Thessalonica, he said he thanked God that the saints had been melted down and put into circulation through faith that works. We work from faith, not for salvation. What on earth are you doing for heaven's sake? Do you have a faith that works?

II. A Love That Labors

Paul then wrote to the Thessalonians, "I not only thank God that you have a faith that works, but I thank God that you have a love that labors." An abused word in our generation is the word *love*. We use that word in many ways. A woman sees a hat and says, "I love that hat." She makes a new dress and says, "I love to sew." We know she is not speaking of the same kind of love.

In the Greek New Testament there are three words commonly used for love. One is the word *eros*. *Eros* is a physical love, a love of passion or sex. A second word for love is *phileo*. It is mental love. It means "brotherly love," the kind of love that one has for a friend. There is a third word for love, *agape*. This refers to God's kind of love, a sacrificing love, the kind of love Christ had when He died on the cross for the sins of the world.

When Paul wrote to the church at Thessalonica, he said, he thanked God for their labor of *agape* love, the kind of love that labors, toils, sacrifices, and sweats for the Master.

John wrote about this love in 1 John 3:16-18:

Hereby perceive we the love of God, because he laid down his life for us: and we ought to lay down our lives for the brethren. But whoso hath this world's good, and seeth his brother have need, and shutteth up his bowels of compassion from him, how dwelleth the love of God in him? My little children, let us not love in word, neither in tongue; but in deed and in truth.

So many people have a love that is only in word, only on their tongues, only in their mouths. They have no love that leaps out and serves and sacrifices.

I'm reminded of the story of the young soldier overseas. He was writing his girlfriend. He wanted to send her a telegram because he thought that would make more of an impression. So he gave the telegraph operator a message to send. The message was this: "I love you. I love you. I love you. John."

The telegraph operator said, "Son, for the same amount of money you can send one more word."

So he amended his message, and it read like this: "I love you. I love you. I love you. Cordially, John."

Many of us profess our love for God, "I love you, I love you, I love you," but when push comes to shove, our devotion is more like "cordially" than it is love.

Vachel Lindsay, the poet, tells of how one day he was caught in the rural section of a community and needed to spend the night. Seeing a large, prosperous-looking farmhouse, he went up and knocked on the door. A man came to the door, and Lindsay said: "Sir, may I come in and spend the night with you and your family? I have no money to pay, but I will recite original poetry for you if you will let me spend the night."

The man replied: "No, I'm sorry; we can't keep you this evening. But if you'll go to that farmhouse across the road, perhaps that man will keep you."

Lindsay left the porch, walked across a field and a road, and knocked on the door of the second house. It was a rundown shack, just two rooms. When the man came to the door, Lindsay repeated his request for lodging.

The man said, "I don't have much, but come in and spend the night."

As Lindsay walked into the room, he observed that there was not a piece of furniture in the house worth more than two dollars. There was only one bed with broken springs. There was not a carpet on the floor, not a drape at the window. It was obvious that the owner was extremely poor.

That night when they sat down to eat, they had a meager fare—no meat, just beans and bread.

But later Lindsay made this profound statement: "That man had nothing and gave me half of it, and we both had an abundance."

That will not work as a mathematical formula, but it will work in the Christian life if the believer will share what he or she has with those who are in need. If the Christian has a love that will roll up its sleeves and labor, God will bless that kind of service.

The parable of the good Samaritan illustrates a love that labors. A man was wounded, half dead. The priest and the Levite, the religious men of the community, passed him by because they had to be at the annual meeting of their religious association. But the Samaritan stopped, rolled up his sleeves, ministered to the man, and took him in to town.

Why did the priest and the Levite not stop? Was it because they did not have enough time or money? No. It was because they did not have enough compassion. When we measure our service or lack of it, we realize that either we love people and are compassionate, or else we dislike people and therefore render no service.

Sometimes we should ask ourselves, "What have I done this week that only a Christian would do in the name of Jesus because I love God and other people?"

III. A Hope That Endures

Melt down the saints and put them into circulation because believers need a hope that is patient and endures.

The word *patient* in the Bible is a meaningful word. It is not a picture of a person sitting in a rocking chair doing nothing. Rather it is a picture of a person seeing a need, laboring with all his or her might to meet that need, and never being discouraged about the outcome. That is the patience of the Scriptures, the kind of patience we need. Paul said the believer needs a hope that endures, a hope that is patient.

When young Alexander the Great made preparation to succeed his father, Philip, he started by giving away everything he had. Finally one of his generals said, "Alexander, you are giving away everything you have."

Alexander responded, "I am giving away everything but hope." With that hope, at the age of thirty-three he had conquered the world. We must never lose our hope!

Do not put ultimate hope in education. Do not rest ultimate hope in science. Do not put ultimate hope in politics. Let us not place our ultimate hope in finances, in ability, or in personality. Let us not build our hopes on armaments, but let us rest our ultimate hope in Jesus Christ. Without Him there is no hope. He is the Christian's ultimate hope!

There is no doubt that Paul was writing in eschatological terms. He was talking about the coming of Jesus Christ. He said when the whole world is as dark as midnight, we should have a hope that endures because we look forward to the coming of Christ.

When the saints are melted down and put into circulation, they have a hope that endures. Paul spoke of that hope in every chapter of the Book of Thessalonians. In chapter 1, "To wait for his Son from heaven, whom he raised from the dead" (v. 10). In chapter 2, "For what is our hope, or joy, or crown of rejoicing? Are not even ye in the presence of our Lord Jesus Christ at his coming?" (v. 19). In chapter 3, "For verily, when we were with you, we told you before that we should suffer tribulation; even as it came to pass, and ye know" (v. 4). In chapter 4, "I would not have you to be ignorant, brethren, concerning them which are asleep, that ye sorrow not, even as others which have no hope" (v. 13). In chapter 5, he predicted the imminent return of our Lord. Paul talked about the hope that we have in Jesus Christ.

Abbi Pierre often uses the phrase, "Penicillin for despair." I agree with him that the world's greatest need is to be brought out of the depths of despair. The only One who can rescue the world from despair is the Lord Jesus Christ. He is the lone ray of hope of a dim, dark horizon. He is our ultimate hope.

Where is our hope? Our hope must ultimately be in Jesus Christ. Paul said we must have the work of faith, the labor of love, and the patience of hope. For the Christian there is always the knowledge that no matter how dark things may be, the bright Morning Star will soon appear. No matter how bad racial tensions may become, Jesus Christ is the ultimate answer. No matter how evil may seem to triumph over good, one day Jesus will come and reign on this earth for one thousand years. We need to look to Jesus, place our faith in Him, and love Him with all our hearts.

Tigranes, king of Armenia, was conquered in a battle with the Romans and, with his wife and children, was taken before the Roman general. The general was about to pronounce the death sentence on the defeated king, his wife, and children. But before making the pronouncement, the general allowed Tigranes an opportunity to speak.

Tigranes fell at the feet of the Roman general and begged: "If you want to put me to death, that's fine. But I plead that you will spare my wife and children and let them go free. Kill me, but spare them."

The Roman general was so moved by this touching display of obvious love for his family that he set the entire family free. As they journeyed away from the Roman camp, the king of Armenia turned to his wife and asked, "Did you see that look on the face of that Roman general as he forgave us and freed us? Did you see it?"

"No, I didn't see it."

"But, how could you have missed it? He gave us our lives!"

The king's wife replied, "I could look only at the man who was willing to die that I might receive life."

If believers could only look at the man Jesus Christ who did die that we might have hope of life eternal! Let us have faith in Him, let us labor in love for Him, and for His sake let us develop a hope that endures.

15
The Final Judgment of the Church

(1 Cor. 3:11—4:5; 2 Cor. 5:10)

Our bomber was on a routine mission over Italy. There was not a cloud in the sky, and visibility was excellent. Everybody on board was keeping their eyes open for enemy fighters or flack. We hit our target, scored a knockout, and were on our way home when, suddenly, out of nowhere the German Messerschmitts came diving upon us. Before we knew it, two of our engines had been shot out, the copilot was dead, and I was doing everything within my power to keep the plane under control. The order was quickly given to bail out. One by one the men plunged from the plane. Before I had an opportunity to jump myself, I suddenly realized that the plane was in a tailspin, and there was nothing I could do. I knew that my life would soon be gone . . . .

This was a story related by an air force pilot during World War II. As he made his descent down toward the earth, many things flashed through his mind. The preacher to whom he was relating the story asked him the question: "As your plane headed toward the earth, and you realized that you were going to crash, about what did you think? Did you think about your family?"

The man replied no.

"Did you think about your friends?"

The man replied no.

"Did you think about the copilot dead by your side?"

"No."

The preacher then asked, "What did you think about when you realized that soon you would die?"

The pilot said very softly and quietly, "As our plane headed toward Earth there was but one thought in my mind. It was the thought that within less than five minutes I would be standing face-to-face with God."

Daniel Webster stated that the most solemn thought he ever had was that one day he would stand before God and give an account of the deeds he had done in the flesh. Perhaps those of us who think seriously find this to be the greatest and most solemn thought we have ever experienced—that one day we will meet God face-to-face.

Many judgments are mentioned in the Bible. The Christian faces at least three. We cannot simply say that salvation is all of grace and go on our way forgetting that we bear a responsibility to God. What a terrible thing it is to make God's grace the occasion for living in sin. Whatever people sow that will they also reap, whether they are Christians or not. Even those of us who are Christians will one day stand before the judgment seat of Christ and give an account of the things done in the flesh, whether they are good or bad. This is the final judgment of the church.

I. Three Judgments of Believers

A. As a Sinner

In A.D. 29 at Calvary where Christ died for our sins, the believer was judged as a sinner. The basis of this judgment was the finished work of Jesus Christ. The result was death as Christ was slain for our transgressions. The second result was life for us as we trusted Him as our personal Savior.

In 1 Peter 2:24 we read, "Who his own self bare our sins in his own body on the tree, that we, being dead to sins, should live unto righteousness: by whose stripes ye were healed." Peter was saying that at the cross of Calvary, our sins were forgiven; and we are healed, not of illness but of sin. Paul reconfirmed the truth that Christians will never stand in a final judgment of condemnation, "There is therefore now no condemnation to them which are in Christ Jesus" (Rom. 8:1).

B. As a Son

Having trusted Christ as personal Savior, the believer has been judged as a sinner and has been forgiven. Now the believer is judged as a son or as a daughter. The moment you accepted Christ as your personal Savior, the sin question was settled forever. But even though the sin question was settled, we are not—nor can we ever be—completely free of the old sin nature. This is sometimes called "natural depravity." It is the tendency that we have to do evil.

Romans 7 describes the conflict that goes on in the believer. On the one hand, we have the flesh, and it lusts, or makes war, against the spirit. We have a natural tendency to sin, and we have the Holy Spirit who tries to lead us to God.

When Christians sin, the Bible says that we have an Advocate with the Father: Jesus Christ, the righteous. John told us, "If we confess our sins, he is faithful and just to forgive us our sins, and to cleanse us from all unrighteousness" (1 John 1:9).

Sometimes believers are like the prodigal son: they determine that they are going to move in opposition to the will of the Heavenly Father. The result is that they find themselves far away from God. The son must return to the Father.

What happens when we stray away from God, when we sin, when we disobey God? These unconfessed sins, if not judged by us, will be judged by God. Paul wrote in 1 Corinthians 11:31-32: "For if we would judge ourselves, we should not be judged. But when we are judged we are chastened of the Lord, that we should not be condemned with the world."

Our duty then, as children of God, is to judge ourselves daily, confess our sins so we may avert the chastisement of the Heavenly Father.

C. As a Servant

Ultimately, you and I are going to be judged as servants of God. This relates itself to the judgment seat of Christ. Remember, at Calvary we were judged as to sin, and our sin was forgiven. In our lives we are judged as sons and daughters of God. If we stay in fellowship with God, there is no problem. If we sin against God, we must repent and confess our sins. Refusing to do this brings the chastisement of God.

One day we will be judged as servants, and this will occur when Christ comes again, at the judgment seat of Christ. Jesus is coming again to resurrect the dead Christians, rapture the living Christians, and the Bible says that at that moment we will be taken into the presence of Christ. We will be judged so that Christ may reward us for what we have done in His service.

II. Three Facts about the Judgment

A. Jesus Christ Will Be the Judge

Paul asked the Roman Christians: "Why doest thou judge thy brother? or why dost thou set at nought thy brother? for we shall all stand before the judgment seat of Christ" (14:10).

Christ will be the Judge at the judgment seat. Paul wrote in 2 Corinthians 5:10, "We must all appear before the judgment seat of Christ; that every one may receive the things done in his body, according to that he hath done, whether it be good or bad."

If Jesus Christ is to be the Judge at the final day of reckoning, let us not presume to take the place of God. The Bible says that we are not to judge one another. Jesus taught, "Judge not, that ye be not judged" (Matt. 7:1). The day will come when Christ will judge us, and His judgment will be fair, impartial, and final.

How often when we judge people, we misjudge them. Eli looked on the outward appearance of Hannah, and by her outward appearance he considered her a drunken woman who had come into the tabernacle. He felt she deserved to be rebuked. What he did not know was the bitterness of her soul, the taunts the polygamous household had heaped on her, and her unseen striving in prayer. He did not comprehend the holy hope that beat within her breast. Eli made a mistake, and he wrongly accused Hannah. His knowledge was imperfect. Not so with Jesus; having all knowledge, possessing all facts, Jesus will be our Judge at the judgment seat of Christ.

You and I have no way of knowing the struggles through which our brothers and sisters go. Some people who are Christians live victorious lives much easier than others who have not had the background of a Christian home or Christian rearing.

Some of us have trouble controlling our tempers. We are like Simon Peter. Others are like John, the beloved apostle. Even after conversion, Peter remained Peter, and John remained John. Peter had a fiery, snappy temper, and John was the loving, quiet disciple. The Bible says, "Judge nothing before the time, until the Lord comes" (1 Cor. 4:5).

Remember, it is a great deal easier for some people to grow in grace and have victory than others. Some work in an ungodly office or shop. Perhaps they have a vulgar husband or wife. The Lord knows all of these things and takes them into account.

It is a great deal easier for a husband who has been blessed with a spiritual, patient, and kind Christian wife to live for God than it is for a husband who has a complaining, bickering, fault-finding, griping mate (or vice versa regarding the wife).

Remember that our environment, our temperament, our circumstances, and our associates all have a bearing on the amount of struggling we are called upon to do. It is not then totally how much we do for Christ, but how much we do with the ability and talent we have. Jesus will be the Judge at the judgment seat of Christ.

B. The Judgment Will Be by Fire

In 1 Corinthians 3:11-15 Paul stated:

> For other foundation can no man lay than that is laid, which is Jesus Christ. Now if any man build upon this foundation gold, silver, precious stones, wood, hay, stubble; Every man's work shall be made manifest: for the day shall declare it, because it shall be revealed by fire; and the fire shall try every man's work of what sort it is. If any man's work abide which he hath built thereupon, he shall receive a reward. If any man's work shall be burned, he shall suffer loss: but he himself shall be saved; yet so as by fire.

Here is a picture of two Christians. Both build on the foundation of Jesus Christ. We can build on no other foundation (v. 11). One person allows God to build his or her work, life ministry, home, business, and personal happiness. The result is that the individual has gold, silver, and precious stones at the judgment. Perhaps the person does not make a big splash in the world. The Christian may not be well known, but the day comes when the fire of God tries his or her work. What does fire do to gold, silver, and precious stones? It refines and purifies.

On the other hand, another Christian also builds on Christ, but this person is ostentatious; his or her works are only for display. This individual wants the world to know what he or she has accomplished. So the Christian builds with wood, hay, and stubble. A great amount of wood, hay, and stubble will not be very valuable.

Wood, hay, and stubble can be grown by people. We can plant forests and get wood. We can cultivate fields and get hay, but the leftover stubble is of little value. The fire tries this Christian's work. What happens when the fire falls on wood, hay, and stubble? They burn; they are lost. So this persons suffers a loss.

Notice what Paul said in verse 15, "If any man's work shall be burned, he shall suffer loss: but he himself shall be saved; yet so as by fire." Christ is going to judge us not just for the deeds we do, but for the motive behind the deeds.

The Bible tells us that He will judge us according to what we have done. But motive is very important. Nobody noticed the poor widow casting in her half penny to the treasury except Christ. But He said she would be rewarded. Nobody noticed Zacchaeus up the "sycomore tree" except Christ. No one seems to mention the infants except Christ, but to Him they are very important.

When someone gives even a cup of cold water in the name of Christ, that person will in no wise lose his or her reward. The smallest, most humble ministries are noted by our Lord.

He sees the sparrow fall, He numbers the hairs on our head, and He tells us that we are of more value than sparrows. Christ is interested in not only what we do, but He wants it to be done with style, with class, or if you please, with a pure motive.

So here we have it: gold, silver, and precious stones; wood, hay, and stubble. One is small compared to the value of the others. One can't stand fire, but purified by the fire.

Wood, hay, and stubble represent the flesh.

Gold, silver, and precious stones represent the Spirit.

Wood, hay, and stubble represent the natural.

Gold, silver, and precious stones represent the supernatural.

Christ is talking about what we do and why we do it. The judgment is one of fire.

C. Christians Will Receive Rewards

"If any man's work abide which he hath built thereupon, he shall receive a reward" (1 Cor. 3:14).

"Do you mean to tell me there are going to be rewards in heaven?" Yes, without a doubt! The Bible mentions at least five crowns that a Christian can win.

1. A crown of life. James promised, "Blessed is the man that endureth temptation: for when he is tried, he shall receive the crown of life, which the Lord hath promised to them that love him" (Jas. 1:12). As Jesus admonished "Be thou faithful unto death, and I will give thee a crown of life" (Rev. 2:10). This is the martyr's crown, here is the crown for those that love Christ. Stephen received that crown as he was stoned to death because of his faithfulness to Christ (Acts 7).

2. The crown of glory. Simon Peter was a faithful minister of Jesus Christ. He was well aware of what the Lord wanted His pastors to do. He admonished those living in his day with these words: "Feed the flock of God which is among you, taking the oversight thereof, not by constraint, but willingly; not for filthy lucre, but of a ready mind; neither as being lords over God's heritage, but being ensamples to the flock. And when the chief Shepherd shall appear, ye shall receive a crown of glory that fadeth not away" (1 Pet. 5:2-4).

This would be the elder's crown, the pastor's crown, or the chief shepherd's crown. It is given to someone who serves not for filthy lucre but simply for the love of the Lord. This is given to the pastor who is not a dictator but who is a faithful and dedicated servant.

This is to a pastor who serves not because he has to but because he wants to. It is called the crown of glory.

Any Christian who serves faithfully in a place of leadership in the church can receive this crown. Here is a deacon chairman, a committee chairman, a departmental director, a teacher, or someone with a responsibility serving in the right spirit. That person serves because he or she loves Jesus. Be faithful. The reward is coming!

3. A crown of righteousness. Even the apostle Paul anticipated the coming of Jesus Christ. He wrote in 2 Timothy 4:8, "Henceforth there is laid up for me a crown of righteousness, which the Lord, the righteous judge, shall give me at that day: and not to me only, but unto all them also that love his appearing."

This is a crown that will be given for personal devotion and love for Jesus Christ. Righteousness means that the individual is right with God and right with others. It means that the heart is filled with love for Jesus and love for others. This individual is thus anticipating the coming of Jesus Christ.

4. The incorruptible crown. Those who are faithful Christians in the church are promised an incorruptible crown. When the Olympic games were held and an individual won a contest, a laurel wreath, a crown of victory, would be placed on the winner's brow. With the passing of time, the leaves would whither and decay. The participant, however, had great joy and pride in the crown that he had won.

The apostle Paul told us that we are in the olympics of life. If we are faithful to Jesus Christ by maintaining a mastery of the body, the result will be the gift of the incorruptible crown. It is possible for a Christian to be so intemperate that he or she loses a place of service. Paul admonished the Corinthian Christians to be faithful to Christ just as a runner is in a race or as a boxer is in a fight. Christians are to so live that we will have places of service in this life and crowns in the life to come (1 Cor. 9:25-27).

5. The crown of rejoicing. The final crown that church members may receive at the judgment is called the crown of rejoicing. Paul told the Thessalonian believers that they were his crown of rejoicing. In other words, he was telling them that he had won them to Christ.

He put it in the form of a question: "For what is our hope, or joy, or crown of rejoicing? Are not even ye in the presence of our Lord Jesus Christ at his coming? For ye are our glory and joy" (1 Thess. 2:19-20).

Throughout the New Testament we read of how the followers of Christ sought to lead others to know the Savior. Andrew brought his own brother, Peter, to Christ. Philip brought the eunuch to Christ. Paul led Dorcas, the Philippian jailer, and many others to Christ. So it is true that you and I should seek to lead others to know Christ as their Savior.

Princess Eugenia of Sweden sold her crown jewels and built a home for incurables. Someone asked her about it, and she said, "I saw the glitter of my diamonds in a woman's tears today."

III. Three Ways to Prepare for the Judgment

A. Be a Worker for Christ (1 Cor. 3:13-15)

The Bible makes it clear that we are to labor for the glory of God. Jesus, our perfect example, encourages us to work for God. He said: "I must work the works of him that sent me, while it is day: the night cometh, when no man can work" (John 9:4). Indeed, when Jesus came to the end of His ministry, He told the Father, "I have finished the work which thou gavest me to do" (John 17:4).

The apostle Paul pointed to the day when the work we have done for our Lord will be revealed. If our motive is pure and our work true, we will be richly rewarded. Conversely, if our motive is selfish and our work false, we as Christians will be saved, but we will suffer loss of reward (1 Cor. 3:14-15).

The inimitable Walter B. Knight delights to tell the story of Sophie, the scrub woman. One day, as she was scrubbing the steps of a large New York City building, a tenant said, "Sophie, I understand that you're a child of God."

"Yes, sir, I'm a child of the King!"

"Well, since you're a child of the King, do you believe that God recognizes you as a princess?"

"He certainly does," beamed Sophie.

"Well, if God is your Father, and if you're a princess and a child of the King, don't you think it is beneath your level to be found here in New York City scrubbing those dirty steps?"

Undaunted, Sophie replied "There's no humiliation whatsoever. You see, I'm not scrubbing these steps for my boss. I am scrubbing them for Jesus Christ, my Savior." Amen! There is a beautiful dignity in the lowest and most menial task that we perform if we are doing it for our precious Savior, Jesus Christ. Be a worker for Christ!

B. Be Faithful to Christ (1 Cor. 4:1-2)

You and I are given life. God refers to us as stewards. That means that we are to carefully manage the time and resources that He has given in our pilgrimage while we are here on the earth. God does not require us to be successful. He does admonish us to be faithful. Regarding the final judgment, Paul stated: "Moreover it is required in stewards, that a man be found faithful."

When Pompeii was destroyed by the eruption of Mount Vesuvius, many persons buried in the ruins were discovered in a variety of positions. Some were found in deep vaults, as if they had gone there for security. Some were found in lofty chambers. But where did they find the Roman sentinel?

They found him standing at the city gate where he had been placed by the captain with his hands still grasping the weapon. There, while the earth shook beneath him, there while the floods of ashes and cinders overwhelmed him, he had stood at his post; and there, after 1,000 years, he was found. So let Christians stand by their duty in their post at which their Captain places them.

C. Be Holy in Christ (1 Cor. 3:16-17)

The Word of God teaches that the body of the Christian is the temple of the living God. Instead of dwelling in temples made with hands, the Spirit of God dwells in the temple of human body. Consequently, we are to keep ourselves undefiled in God's presence (1 Cor. 3:16).

The Christian should be clean inside and outside. In this life if we defile our bodies, illness usually follows, and even death can result

(1 Cor. 3:17). We must always remember that our bodies are holy. There will also be an accounting of what we have done in our bodies in the life to come. We should never deceive ourselves by being proud and haughty. We are to be holy and humble (1 Cor. 3:18).

Dr. Lewis Evans tells of a man who entered the hut of a British officer in Africa and found his friend clad in a dinner jacket and before him the appointments of formal dinner. Surprised at this dressing for dinner in the midst of a lot of African savages, the friend expressed fear of the officer's sanity. But he received the explanation that once a week the custom of dressing for dinner was followed because the officer felt that he must not adopt the customs and standards of the natives of Africa. He belonged to the empire of Britain, and he determined to live according to the codes of British conduct no matter how his heathen neighbors lived. So also Christians belong to a different empire. They are called unto a life of holiness because God is holy. Their behavior patterns are to be taken from Christ, not the world. Ours is the high calling of God in Christ Jesus, and one day all people will give account of themselves to God. Be a worker for Christ; be faithful to Christ; be holy in Christ. Jesus will reward you richly at the judgment of believers.